Really Fake

IN SEARCH OF MEDIA

Timon Beyes, Mercedes Bunz, and Wendy Hui Kyong Chun, Series Editors

Really Fake

Alexandra Juhasz, Ganaele Langlois,
and Nishant Shah

IN SEARCH OF MEDIA

University of Minnesota Press
Minneapolis
London

meson press

Joseph Entin, "Experimental Escape Routes Needed: One Block," published by permission. Anonymous, "Contrived moment," published by permission. Nina Daro, Mahalia Hughes-Roussel, and Allison Rapp, "Moving," published by permission. Anonymous, "How do we best make fun of power?" published by permission. M. Astley, "do not be distracted from the truth," published by permission. Poets of Course, "Technology is a Weapon" published by permission of Harvey P. Kyle Booten, "for we understood their suffering, didn't we?" published by permission.

In Search of Media is a collaboration between the University of Minnesota Press and meson press, an open access publisher, https://meson.press

Really Fake by Alexandra Juhasz, Ganaele Langlois, and Nishant Shah is licensed under a Creative Commons Attribution-NonCommercial 4.0 International License.

Published by the University of Minnesota Press, 2021
111 Third Avenue South, Suite 290
Minneapolis, MN 55401-2520
https://www.upress.umn.edu

in collaboration with
meson press
Salzstrasse 1
21335 Lüneburg, Germany
https://meson.press

ISBN 978-1-5179-1101-0 (pb)
A Cataloging-in-Publication record for this book is available from the Library of Congress.

The University of Minnesota is an equal-opportunity educator and employer.

Contents

Series Foreword

"Media determine our situation," Friedrich Kittler infamously wrote in his Introduction to *Gramophone, Film, Typewriter.* Although this dictum is certainly extreme—and media archaeology has been critiqued for being overly dramatic and focused on technological developments—it propels us to keep thinking about media as setting the terms for which we live, socialize, communicate, organize, do scholarship, et cetera. After all, as Kittler continued in his opening statement almost thirty years ago, our situation, "in spite or because" of media, "deserves a description." What, then, are the terms—the limits, the conditions, the periods, the relations, the phrases—of media? And, what is the relationship between these terms and determination? This book series, *In Search of Media,* answers these questions by investigating the often elliptical "terms of media" under which users operate. That is, rather than produce a series of explanatory keyword-based texts to describe media practices, the goal is to understand the conditions (the "terms") under which media is produced, as well as the ways in which media impacts and changes these terms.

Clearly, the rise of search engines has fostered the proliferation and predominance of keywords and terms. At the same time, it has changed the very nature of keywords, since now any word and pattern can become "key." Even further, it has transformed the very process of learning, since search presumes that, (a) with the right phrase, any question can be answered and (b) that the answers lie within the database. The truth, in other words, is "in there." The impact of search/media on knowledge, however, goes beyond search engines. Increasingly, disciplines—from sociology to economics, from the arts to literature—are in search of media as a way to revitalize their methods and objects of study. Our current media situation therefore seems to imply a new term, understood as temporal shifts of mediatic conditioning. Most broadly, then, this series asks: What are the terms or conditions of knowledge itself?

To answer this question, each book features interventions by two (or more) authors, whose approach to a term—to begin with: *communication, pattern discrimination, markets, remain, machine, archives, organize, action at a distance, undoing networks*—diverge and converge in surprising ways. By pairing up scholars from North America and Europe, this series also advances media theory by obviating the proverbial "ten year gap" that exists across language barriers due to the vagaries of translation and local academic customs and in order to provoke new descriptions, prescriptions, and hypotheses—to rethink and reimagine what media can and must do.

Introduction

Alexandra Juhasz and Nishant Shah

In the summer of 2019, Wendy Chun set up Alexandra Juhasz and Nishant Shah. We met over fish sandwiches and cokes in a tiny restaurant on a quiet tree-lined canal in Amsterdam. The conversation was lively, jumping electrically from scholarly ideas to mutual friends, flirtatious banter, academic politics. It was a great first date, and they agreed, as Alex left hastily to return to her scholarly summer school in digital methods, to meet again soon.

In November 2019 that came to pass. Alex flew to Arnhem, where Nishant works at ArtEZ University of the Arts, and things continued just where they had left off. Over four heady, almost fevered days, their passionate connection inspired something new: the two interlaced, interdependent essays you find here.

Although they barely knew each other, and their intense intimacy at times might have felt forced, as feminist queer scholars and activists engaged with digital culture, the new couple sprinted to common understandings by sharing meals, words, walks, and stories. To see them through this process was a set of other promiscuous networked relationships—past experiences of collaborating, of co-creating, of trusting the other with ideas and running away with the inspiration that they gave and took from each other.

They quickly and excitedly created a rubric and a set of touchstones that would guide their thinking, as well as twelve subheadings that would inform and link their shared but discrete projects, work that would come from two individuals, in two countries, over what would be a few more months of labor. As their intellectual, political, and writerly commitments informed and joined, they patted each other on the backs. They grinned with delight. "Look we share!" Underneath that grinning exclamation was a reassuring realization. We dare to share because we care. About the task at hand, about each other, and about all the many connections that were coming together in this making.

A Rubric to Guide and Link Our Thinking
Life ≠ Spectacle

Bereft of memory / Abundant in storage

Perched on indeterminacy

Moving in/out of storage

Making dated precious

Virality is virility

Fakeness can be unstuck

Who contrives the moment?

It is not fake if it fools you

Old-fashioned ways of doing things

Something weird happened to time

Individual truths—collective fakes

Measure of bodies that measure up

Underlining, and actually grounding these attachments was a profound vulnerability and linked care. The feminist principles they were attending to with ideas and developing words and lists were reinforced by bodily interactions. During Alex's visit, Nishant had become ill enough that he was shuttling from appointment to appointment, getting screened, poked, tested for what was to be diagnosed as a serious cancer. He wrote his part of the book while dealing with a brutal but life-saving course of treatments.

FAKE	
Touchstones	**Actors**
Tactics	Author
Production	Audience
Reception	Mentor
Resistance	Instigator
Operations	Critic
Infrastructure	Developer
Context	Catalyst
Aesthetic	User

He was recovering in the midst of the global pandemic, whereas Alex, now back in Brooklyn, suffered a mild but prolonged and disturbing bout of COVID-19. Their WhatsApp interactions lived as the ideas of the book in practice: situated bodily care as feminist digital method. A new kind of dating. A new kind of making. A making stretched over countries, continents, health, and safety. A making punctuated by anxiety, worry, fear, and breakdowns.

This small book is a mark of these attachments; a product of intensity of connection; an outcome of short, vivid, enduring, and generative dates. It is a way to do time, together, differently, as humans. It is queer feminist praxis about the same.

Juhasz and Shah situate their unique but linked analyses of internet fakes in local experience, collective art practices, and private photographs and memories. They exhibit and call for human responses to digital malfeasance. Taking up a shared political standpoint, while mining and speaking from two diverse discursive identities, they enact a cyberfeminist commitment to time, people, truth, and their technologies. Feminist internet dating.

Shah and Juhasz ask and try to render queer feminist methods and forms to better reconcile human experiences of time, place, the other, and knowledge with digital versions of the same. To do so Juhasz and Shah use and consider story, poetry, storage, and memory. They rely on old-fashioned feminist commitments to analyze and model a new form of being: Really Fake. That is, being human in a world of storage.

Shah and Juhasz salvage the fake from its current illicit holdings in "fake news," and rejuvenate it as a place of human instability and indeterminacy. Juhasz and Shah refuse to follow the logics of patriarchal networks and corporate violence. What emerges are interrelated efforts: a generation of empathy, a catalysis of responsibility, and a call for feminist internet time as driven by fakes and their underlying bodily, placed, and time-stamped realities.

> Not all fake stories are lies.
> Not all lies are fake truths.
> Not all real stories are true.
> Not all truths are innocent of fakeness.

Faking It until It's Real

Ganaele Langlois

In the winter of 2020, Wendy Chun and Alex Juhasz sent me an early draft of the *Really Fake* manuscript, and asked if I could provide some kind of response for the piece. While Nishant and Alex's collaborative work speaks for itself, here are some contextual thoughts.

Let's take the shouts of "FAKE!" resonating in all corners of our networked life seriously, that is, as the symptoms of the new fascist condition spreading all over the world. The premise for Alex Juhasz and Nishant Shah is that "FAKE!" is a new form of communicative fascism: a dynamic where interpersonal and nonphysical forms of violence have not only multiplied but also been deployed as weapons of mass destruction that leave invisible, yet deep, psycho-social wounds. The kind of insidious violence at play with "just words" being thrown like bombs is both an old and new kind of what Maurizio Lazzarato and Éric Alliez (2018) call the wars against subjectivities, against women and against minorities. Public shaming and ostracization by revealing somebody a FAKE! to their peers and therefore as one that should be trusted by no one is an old trick, common among those whose social development was, to put it mildly, deeply impacted by junior high school. "FAKE!" is also old, because just like the husband in the eponymous movie who covertly and subtly manipulates gaslights in the house to make his spouse go insane, the questioning of someone's handle on reality—that what they experience is fake and therefore that they are insane and should not trust themselves—is a common trick in the domestic abuser's toolkit. Whether FAKE! is meant to destabilize one's self-integrity or to destroy trust in the world out there, the aim is the same: to atomize individuals through severing social bonds and to destroy our capacity to care, to be curious, to engage.

FAKE! is never about truth, it's about domination. FAKE! is the mainstream media, which should really be understood not as an attack on traditional news sources as the epitome of the fourth estate in Western democracies but rather as a severing of the spaces of mediations—biased and limited as they may have been—that enabled the crafting of some form of collective imaginaries and social bonds that could extend beyond already established communities and into the unknown, the different, the heterogenous. Not only are messages FAKE! but so are the mediators and messengers—the institutions and the people representing them, from journalists to teachers to professors, teenage survivors of mass shootings and victims of police violence: whatever comes out of their mouth, regardless of its facticity and veracity, therefore cannot be true.

The Trump presidency and the clones that have reduplicated and adapted his communicative warfare strategy all over the world are agents of destruction through deconstruction. What used to be the strategy of the leftist intellectuals—the argument that most values that we believe absolutely true, objective, and unchanging are actually socially and culturally constructed—is now turned against itself. This is first sign of what I call existential gaslighting, where the logic at play is that of false equivalencies: everything is constructed, therefore everything is a lie. Social justice is a construct, therefore social justice is a lie. Further: good is bad; better is worse; empathy is selfish hypocrisy; and any social, political, or economic efforts to address inequalities, limited though they may be, constitute new forms of exploitation against white males everywhere, who are now threatened and at risk. From false equivalencies, we now enter the realm of ontological reversal, the result being that whatever common ground existed has now been replaced by an existential abyss. Not only do we no longer have a common language to share the name of things, people, and values; what we are faced with is an antilanguage that undermines, destroys, and kills the very nature of being as potentiality, creativity, and reaching out for relations to otherness.

Therefore: communicative fascism posits that what is real is the opposite of social justice, and we now see the armies of "Social Injustice Warriors," as Sarah Sharma (2019) calls them, busy typing away at their keyboards to defend their rights to keep their fear of Others unchallenged and to protect their bigotry, misogyny, and racism from being debunked as inept constructions themselves. It is interesting to note that the only emotions that are not fake, according to the new communicative fascism, are fear and rage— the very emotions that fuel further division and undo social bonds and collective imaginaries. Thus, existential gaslighting is not just turned outward but also inward. There is indeed a discipline to the social injustice warrior: fear and rage need to be cultivated and carefully fed. This new anti-care of the self (Foucault 1986) demands a consistent maintenance of one's filter bubbles, a solid regime of fake and misinformed news consumption to feed one's prejudices and avoid anything that could trouble the new fascist narrative, and a dedicated cultivation of a false self (Winnicott 1982) that denies doubts, complexity, and curiosity in order to achieve complete subsumption to the fascist group.

The first aspect of this new communicative fascism is related to what can be called "real fakes," that is to say, the construction of a fictional and alternative reality where the paranoid position of fear and rage can find some validation. The real fake is productive and partakes in a new media aesthetics and logic based on networked virality and virtual reconstruction. Take, for instance, completely unbelievable fake news and conspiracy theories, such as reports of a pedophile ring run by high-profile Democrats and operating out of a pizza restaurant in Washington, D.C., complete with forensics of buried email clues, pictures of the restaurant, and so on. Such stories are as much about content as they are about mimicking a newsworthy format. Such stories as well—and this is part of a long history of how rumors function—are shared and believed not because they are factually true but because they offer a worldview that justifies, in this case, constant fear and mistrust of governing elites and paranoia around being abandoned and left to fend for one's self and family. It has been noted that the more fake information is debunked, the more it tends to be shared (Nyhan and Reifler 2010) and felt by some to be authentic. Real fakes are about what reality *ought* to be: they are the virtual backgrounds on which fascist affects can find their validity and raison d'être. In other words, the readiness to prefer to believe that the entire world is wrong, rather than one's own perceptions, has now found a set of media practices: the massaging of new alternative realities. This aspect of the communicative fascism deploys a post-9/11 media arsenal to preempt (Elmer and Renzi 2012) and premediate events (Grusin 2010) and to massage reality into a specific vision of constant struggle, social abandonment, and glorification of absolute self-reliance and self-interest. But this can only work if there is an affective contagion, that is, if enough people believe the alternate reality to be the actual real one.

Therefore, the second aspect of this new communicative fascism is that it draws from cult-recruitment strategies: promoting a safe and pure vision of what reality should be while offering techniques for brainwashing any doubt or questioning or critical assessment of the solutions being offered. In other words, it's about faking it until it becomes real through instilling fervor in embracing a vision of things to come. This fervor is crucial to in turn negate actual trust in the potential for finding goodness in the world out there. The key, however, is that the safe and pure vision of communicative fascism, built as it is on false equivalencies, is anything but safe and pure. I like to think about the ideal behind the self-disciplined Social Injustice Warrior through the figure of a Toxic Antigone: whereas the original Antigone fought for absolute justice against the hypocrisy of a ruler more concerned with maintaining both social peace and his own popularity, the figure of Toxic Antigone attacks any social justice and equity project as a construction and therefore a lie, rooting himself not in an ideal of universal and pure justice but rather pure right to injustice. It is with this precise moment of living alongside the existential abyss that Alex Juhasz

and Nishant Shah start: how do we pick up the pieces and heal the
wounds of communicative fascism?

The answer so far has been a renewed commitment to truth, to fact, to logical explanation, to transparency. But even when faced with a situation of undeniable fact-ness, the logic of fake and its relationship with the real only reinvents itself: again, fake is never about the truth, it is about the articulation of power over the immaterial—thoughts, feelings, psychic factors—and control over the material—how to bend the world to one's will, how to create a new reality. While dispiriting, it comes as no surprise, as I am writing these words while three billion human beings are currently under Covid-19 lockdown, that the logics of real fake has never quite paused: real fakes abound to try to preempt Covid-19 and its socioeconomic consequences, to control and shape them by, among other tactics, creating alternate realities to explain the current situation. First, it was not a serious virus but a kind of bad cold; then it was invented for nefarious reasons in a lab somewhere; then it became, according to the delusional Trumpian logic, a "Chinese virus" that therefore had no place in his alternative U.S. reality; et cetera, et cetera. Beyond these head-shaking and criminally irresponsible declarations of the fascist mindset as it encounters something truly not controllable without social bonds, trust, and truth (e.g., a pandemic), we have to realize that the virtual real of the fake—the proclamation of what ought to be—fails precisely because it cannot build shared imaginaries (Jasanoff and Kim, 2015).

The concept of the imaginary is inseparable from the practice of building and maintaining social bonds through time and space, that is to say, the constant work of building supportive networks among beings who, while mostly strangers to each other, craft the same values and desires for helpful and empowering connections to create potentials for the emergence of resilient ways of being in the world and in relation to each other. The imaginary is transindividual (Stiegler 2012): it arises through the circulation and sharing of thoughts, ideas, and practices among individuals and collectives and is always an evolving projection about what life together could be like. While traditionally associated with the rise of the idea of the nation-state (Anderson 2006), imaginaries go beyond political recuperation: they are about fostering trust in the capacity to survive and thrive together, which includes not only humans but also nonhuman beings and entities. The real fake, however, built as it is not only on a series of false equivalencies but also on rupturing links with social practices, fosters the opposite of an imaginary, even though it proposes a vision. How, then, do we rebuild the capacity to imagine together a common world?

The first part of the answer lies in exploring the question of the industrialization of subjectivation and the technologies and techniques that accompany them (Sampson 2020). It is clearer now that fascist subjectivation does not only work at the level of conscious cognition as alternative facts, biased knowledge, and false information but even more deeply at the level of the unconscious and nonconscious, targeting specific affects such as rage and fear, framing relational projections through the lens of paranoia and deep mistrust, and creating daily media habits (Chun 2016) that anchor these conscious, nonconscious and unconscious processes in all aspects of life. The new industry of fascist subjectivation is all the more dangerous as it makes use of a sophisticated and global infrastructure of automated targeted personalization hosted on social media platforms (Wooley and Howard 2018) to hijack the ensemble of processes through which we define ourselves as individuals and community members, aiming for a total equivalence between the fabricated fascist subject position and one's sense of self. How can we, then, reinvest in the space of becoming to ourselves and to others in order to reconstruct it as a shared space of potentials?

The starting point, as Alex Juhasz states in the first page of her essay, is fairly straightforward though far from easy: through a reasserted commitment to ethics of care, to relational growth and nurturing. Further, as Alex Juhasz and Nishant Shah illustrate, social construction has never been a lie and should be understood as a project of collective, care-full, and ethical transformation. The

crucial error made by many postmodern intellectuals was to see
social construction as a language game. The reality is that social
construction is co-construction: it requires ethical commitment
and practice. It demands situationality and embodiment, but also
a relational commitment to others and to the world, and requires
accepting that one will inevitably be changed: in other words, it is
about transformation through constant discovery and rediscovery,
through acknowledgment that things are indeed and have always
been in flux. It is the attempt to solidify the world, self, and others
into distinct and separate categories, and the misguided and
dangerous calls for some kind of purified state of being that has
always been the problem.

The challenge, however, is about how to reinvest in this very commitment that is constantly targeted and under attack, denounced
as the core of the FAKE! Nishant Shah and Alex Juhasz both call
for a renewed commitment to community and lived and experienced relationships with others. At the same time, though, such
reinvestment is also crucially mediated and networked. It requires
confronting the very communication system that has enabled
the rise of communicative fascism. Many at this point have been
dreaming of and searching for a fix, of setting up an automated
system that will clean up global and instantaneous communication networks' toxicity through better fact-checking and better
accountability systems for users. But overall, the result is that the
toxicity continues and reinvents itself through new networks as
they move elsewhere to other platforms. The few instances of
successful deplatforming might prevent further publicity for some
neofascist microcelebrities, but the problem is that communicative
fascism striving on paranoia, has established ideological enclosures
and filter bubbles that render impossible any form of exchange.
Further, the digital networked infrastructure that enables the
storage of immense amount of information and instantaneous
communication has offered communicative fascism its capacity for
virality, in particular the repetition and propagation of existential
gaslighting techniques throughout all network nodes. As well,

this infrastructure has provided for the further industrialization of communicative fascism, translating the social into hermetic communities of the same—what Wendy Chun calls "homophily networks" that cut off any heterogeneity or difference. Finally, the contemporary digital infrastructure is thoroughly oriented toward monetizing, mobilizing, and manipulating the psycho-social world of attention, affect, cognition, and habit regardless of the damage that such operations do.

Addressing communicative fascism means necessarily dealing with this communicative infrastructure, but not by trying to "fix" the system. Rather, as Alex Juhasz and Nishant Shah show, we should commit to gestures of engagement other than the ones inscribed within the dominant digital infrastructure. To cite Deleuze: "Creating has always been something different from communicating. The key thing might be to create vacuoles of noncommunication, circuit breakers, so that we can elude control" (1990, 175). To build on this: the key is to question the equivalences, as Warren Sacks call them, between relational gestures and their fabricated and thoroughly artificial digital rendering within networks. Realizing the artificiality of equivalences—that, for instance, care cannot just be a thin line linking two data nodes—is the starting point from which creation of new potentials can start. Hence, the examination of new paradoxes: for instance, while the digital infrastructure might be able to track and record every detail of every moment, it is still completely incapable of rendering lived, felt, and shared relationalities. This is not to argue for a total refusal of communication systems but rather for the need for playfulness with communication systems that always claim to be perfect solutions for frictionless, smooth, and untroubled communication. Poking holes in these claims allows for a renewed sense of attentive and careful playfulness toward the "small events," as Agnes Varda states, that "reconcile us with the world."

"I can't breathe," Bifo titles the first chapter of his latest book, referring to Eric Garner's last sentence when suffocated to death by an NYPD officer. Bifo further states: "In many ways, these words express the general sentiment of our times: physical and psychological breathlessness everywhere, in the megacities choked by pollution, in the precarious social conditions of the majority of exploited workers, in the pervading of violence, war, and aggression" (Bernardi 2019, 15). Alex Juhasz and Nishant Shah's book offers moments of breathing, allowing us to start paying attention again rather than be engulfed in the flows of communicative fascism. I hope the reader will enjoy these small moments of being breathed back to life: through group poetry sessions, through letting our intimate relations unfold through mediated memories, through playfulness with the small incidents that disrupt the smoothness of digital networked flows of information, through a return to mediated yet embodied co-presence.

References

Alliez, Éric, and Maurizio Lazzarato. 2018. *Wars and Capital,* trans. A. Hodges Semiotext(e).

Anderson, Benedict. 2006. *Imagined communities: Reflections on the Origin and Spread of Nationalism.* London: Verso Books.

Berardi, F. "Bifo." 2019. *Breathing: Chaos and Poetry.* Los Angeles: Semiotext(e).

Chun, W. H. K. 2016. *Updating to Remain the Same: Habitual New Media.* Cambridge, Mass.: MIT Press.

Deleuze, Gilles. 1997. *Negotiations, 1972–1990.* trans. M. Joughin New York: Columbia University Press.

Elmer, G., and A. Renzi, eds. 2012. *Infrastructure Critical: Sacrafice at Toronto's G8/G20 Conference.* Winnipeg: Arbeiter Ring Publishing.

Grusin, Richard. 2010. *Premediation: Affect and Mediality after 9/11*. London: Palgrave Macmillan.

Jasanoff, Sheila, and Sang-Hyun Kim, eds. 2015. *Dreamscapes of Modernity: Sociotechnical Imaginaries and the Fabrication of Power.* University of Chicago Press.

Nyhan, Brendan, and Jason Reifler. 2010. "When Corrections Fail: The Persistence of Political Misperceptions." *Political Behavior* 32, no. 2: 303–30.

Sampson, Tony D. 2020. *A Sleepwalker's Guide to Social Media.* Cambridge, UK: Polity.

Sharma, Sarah. 2019. *The Way of the Social Injustice Warrior—100 Years of Now Journal.* Accessed March 30, 2020. https://journal.hkw.de/en/the-way-of-the-social -injustice-warrior/.

Stiegler, B. 2012. "Relational Ecology and the Digital Pharmakon." *Culture Machine* 13. http://www.culturemachine.net/index.php/cm/article/viewDownloadInterstitial /464/496.

Winnicott, D. W. 1982. *Playing and Reality* Abingdon: Routledge.

Woolley, S. C., and P. N. Howard eds. 2018. *Computational Propaganda: Political Parties, Politicians, and Political Manipulation on Social Media*. Oxford: Oxford University Press.

2

Who Contrives the Moment? On Cyberfeminist Dating

Alexandra Juhasz

Preface: Some Foundations, Counts, and Histories of Cyberfeminist Dating

The following twelve sections are episodes in feminist internet dating. I use time, writing, and connection differently to connect people, data, representation, truth, and fakes. These twelve written encounters bring together two bodies of critical production— creatively, hopefully, intensely: seventy or so citations mapping foundational theories of cyberfeminism and seven poems about fake news. These interactions enact an old-fashioned commitment to contemporary technologies, including eight photographs and twenty-six footnotes, nine of which point to the words of my writing partner in the pages of this shared effort. Furthermore, my twelve sections are also matched, sometimes harmoniously, sometimes awkwardly, with writing under the same name by my book-date, Nishant.

Unlike critical internet studies writ large or its burgeoning set of digital methods,[1] cyberfeminism, like many feminisms (and there are many), puts our goals, processes, and bodies first: research in service of making and changing the world, and the internet, for ourselves, feminists, and others.[2] Learned from those before and with me (Sayers 2018; Zarzycka and Olivieri 2017), my cyberfeminism is first and foremost a *method of doing well and for the better* (Ahmed 2016; Gajjala 2019). It is hard to do (well) but easy enough to name (Fernández 2002; Daniels 2009), and naming it up front is part of its best practices (@riotmango; Subrosa). Mine is *situated*: attending to the specificity of its place, time, and author(s) (Carpio 2019; Harpold and Philip 2010); and in this way *committed*: serving and driven by self- and world-changing goals (Losh and Wernimont 2018); *connected and interactive*: rooted in what humans and machines can build and do collectively (Braidotti 2012; Cardenas 2012); and *ethical*: while always attending to intensity and control between people and technologies (Laurel 2003; Nelson 2016); and thus rooted in *care* (McLeod, Rault, and Cowan 2014; Fotopoulou, Juhasz, and O'Riordan 2014), given all the attendant violence (Malkowski and Russworm 2017; FemTechNet).

In my own cyberfeminist practice, I attempt to do what we theorize. For example, I have been engaged for over four years in a transforming, multi-sited project committed to radical digital media literacy. This began during the first hundred days of the Trump administration as an act of enraged and engaged public citizenship, research, pedagogy, and outcry. Its first iteration was the #100hardtruths-#Fakenews[3] primer on digital media literacy. There, I shared a hundred "hardtruths" from whence an ethical, educated populace might take steps to engage with a growing crisis of deceit, uncertainty, and violence rendered in the wake of building confusion.

My commitment to engage arose from decades of work on and in fake media. Previous bodies of work—specifically, the first African American lesbian feature film, the fake documentary *The Watermelon Woman* (Cheryl Dunye, 1996), for which I was producer and actor, and all that followed; and my extensive work on YouTube (2011)—were being challenged by the uncertainties and changes

12   within the crisis of fake news. This sense of challenge seemed to be true for my colleagues in this and related fields (boyd 2017). So, over those initial hundred days, I rethought, researched, and reached out to colleagues and mentors for guidance and sustenance. The online primer holds resources, truisms, art, tools, photos, words of wisdom or confusion, traces of encounter, and much more. But once it was completed and given its internet home, as well as the contradictory truths I had learned about engaging with fake news on the internet—fake news r us[4]—I understood that all this work was only a first step, a resource of resources toward the radical digital media literacy that was needed given that fact of fake news.

I sought methods of being, ways of knowing, and norms of interaction with logics outside of those that buttress the internet: a place and its things that fuel and are fueled by fakes. How could I get to the really fake in this overly fake place? An attempt to do the internet differently inspired me to conceptualize and then run twenty-plus (and counting) Fake News Poetry Workshops around the world as well as a website (fakenews-poetry.org), produce a small book of poems, *My phone lies to me* (Juhasz forthcoming), and release a podcast, *We Need Gentle Truths for Now,* to hold and make use of them during the first wave of the COVID-19 pandemic and lockdown. The workshops were held with local and diverse, small and principled communities and their poets, who chose to so engage. I will share and learn from seven of these poems here, given that I have come to believe that poetry, like stories, are time-honored truth regimes well fit for the expression of our knowledge, disdain, hopes, and plans for the internet. Poems are one method to see the Really Fake. The poets whose work I will cite here are young and old, artists and students, disabled and abled, queer, black, trans, British, indigenous, female, and concerned citizens all. Online, you can see photos of these and more people who wrote fake news poetry, and other associated ephemera from each distinct workshop. For both Nishant and myself, poetry and story, as well as photography (as you will soon see), as well as and then

[Figure 2.1]. Alex Juhasz with Agnès Varda, 2017. "We have to be minimalist. A small event, if we can understand it, reconciles us a little bit with the world." Agnès Varda. For more words of wisdom by Agnès Varda see Kline 2015. Photograph: Alexandra Juhasz.

again, love, will be at the heart of the writerly practices of internet dating that follow.

1. Measure of Bodies That Measure Up

My online primer of digital media literacy and I are left more complete from the wisdom and memories of human encounters, even if some of this must also go lost. Agnès Varda died March 29, 2019. In conversation with her ideas, on March 9, 2017, I claimed "#37, size matters; we have to be minimalist."[5]

How do we counter the prevailing norms and systems that produce and escalate the crisis of fakeness? Let's start with scale. If we measure a fake with cyberfeminist rubrics and tactics—as big as and no bigger than my body and the worlds, commitments, humans, and machines it can hold and is held by—we can render experimental escape routes, like poetry, built to a human scale of space and time

14   (Barad 2007), be that vast and imaginative, or perhaps just as big as one block.

Experimental Escape Routes Needed: One Block

Muriel Rukeyser tells us: "Poetry can extend the
    document."
How does one document a neighborhood? What
    kind of poetics are required?
Neighborhoods occur at different scales:
The house, the stoop, the street, the quarter.
Where I live, life is block by block.
The block is a container
The block is a party
The block is a conflict
The block is a city
The block is an outrage
The block is a safehouse
The block is a trap
The block is being undone
The block is being rebuilt
The block is mine
The block is theirs
The block is filthy
The block is a history
The block is this tree, this stone, this door, this
    flag, this poem.

—Joseph Entin, Fake News Poetry Workshop,
Brooklyn College, 2019[6]

Blocks, like people and their movements, are made up of different scales: parties, conflicts, cities, and outrage. Fake News Poetry Workshops, and the poems that they render, are cyberfeminist processes that make and take some time and space for the knowledge, feelings, and truths of humans.

2. Bereft of Memory, Abundant in Storage

There are approaches to *dates* and *datedness* that can be useful for thinking about and doing differently fakes. Attending to time through attention to the details of specific situations and places that are held in it can set into play human returns to the richness of memory and our vital encounters with people otherwise lost.

Give me a moment to get there. In Spring 2019, I decided to reboot one of my dormant critical internet studies courses, Feminist Online Spaces (femininstonlinespaces.com). It felt like the right time (again) to think about and with scholarly internet feminism. However, given 2019's immense volume of popular (internet) feminism, perhaps reaching some sort of crescendo and certainly loud enough to obscure or simply subsume all other feminist (internet) forms, the class was already sort of *dated.* Rather suddenly (as is the way with internet time), a feminist online space had somehow suddenly come to be. This felt like a big surprise after several decades of cyberfeminism having yielded what felt like barely a toehold (Post-Cyber Feminist International 2017).

Some quick internet research on my own course site established that the last time I had taught it had been six years previously, in August 2013. In its first two iterations, I had worked with undergrads where I used to teach in the suburbs of Los Angeles, at the Claremont Colleges. This time, I taught the course with Masters students in Liberal Studies (MALS) at the CUNY Graduate Center in Manhattan.

Teaching the class in spring 2019—within a website that kept the Feminist Online Spaces of 2011 and 2013 fixed and at our disposal—one particular problem became clear. Time was to become our central, consistent, and defining companion and complaint. The trouble was borne from the persisting data of past classes in all their digital, available abundance. This was a time trouble expressed glibly. Its commonsense shorthand was a universally felt fixation on and disdain for the recent past's goofy technologies, stilted vernaculars, naive norms, and immaterial peoples. I was challenged by my students' heartfelt, near-constant complaint about being assigned to engage with such *dated* materials and questions about the internet (Why don't women code? or "When we are online, what is real, and by corollary, what is fake?"[7]). I was forced to reckon with competing temporalities: my own, where I felt like six to ten years was a blip in my lifetime, not to mention within any scholarly tradition; and that of my students, who could barely deign to lay their eyes on previous classwork given that the terminology, technologies, practices, and critical assumptions therein were so *dated.*

The stupid unknowing recent digital past haunted the class and made us all agitated: it was *too* different. We hadn't heard of Trump or even Twitter. The words scholars used with such hip flippancy in the books that we read for class (Gray 2010; Coleman 2011; Gajjala and Oh 2012; Nakamura and Chow-White 2012; Gordon and Mihailidis 2016; Banet-Weiser 2018) were utterly, laughingly outré (the Net! cyberspace? MOOC?!). And websites, well, they looked downright silly. They all seemed stuck in yesteryear's embarrassing fonts, formats, and interfaces. People's moods were *impossible* (hopeful, utopian). Founding assumptions were inapt or seemingly fatuous: women *not* being on the internet? An expressed interest in *potentially* using digital media to engage with electoral politics! *Really?* Nostalgia was expressed for only a few very specific times or more accurately things: those that were *dated* but also somehow cute; the images, websites, and activities of the proto-digital '90s (Neopets or Myspace), or the sweet old aughts (when my students were young). "Forgetting allows for us to move forward,"[8] writes my book-date Nishant Shah elsewhere in this volume, one of nine such interlacings created by learning from and then sharing each other. But, anything much closer seemed of no use at all, gross examples of internet time-trash.

When and why had things sped up and slowed down so? In her book on temporality and cultural politics, *In the Meantime,* Sarah Sharma explains how "individuals and groups synchronize their

body clocks, their senses of the future or the present, to an exterior
relation" (2014, 18). These 2019 feminist graduate students—like
me, like all of us—had come (just recently?) to synchronize our
body clocks to some new exterior relation—*internet time*—which
seemed to be causing a shared, compelling disdain for almost any
digital thing except for its zooming blooming now.

There is no future, the past is insignificant, the present blips and
bleeps and swipes and sweeps and can't and won't stick (it's built
not to), and we don't either. The screen is the time, it is all that
matters, it has no matter. We have become unstuck as a matter of
words and toys. But don't get me wrong: the effects are monumen-
tal. Valuable things and people seem and thus become immaterial.
Internet time has accordioned with and (de-) and (re)accelerated in
ways that have changed teaching, feminism, humans, and the internet. Internet time hurtles at the pace of memes and makes its and
our own recent past seem irrelevant, ham-fisted, embarrassing.

But could we inhabit this too-familiar internet sensation differently
by heeding cyberfeminist principles and methods: refocusing our
attention to times and places at the human scale of our internal
and interpersonal clocks rather than those produced by the
patriarchal logics of the corporate, government, and viral (Keeling
2019)? How could we trouble datedness's push to forget, disdain,
and keep in constant motion rather than in connection? Could
we make better use of the internet's extraordinary capacities for
writers and researchers to mark (timestamp) the lived presentness
of our flowing and building digital voice? Could we attend to the
specific (if always changing) concerns and contexts linking time and
its places (Dean 2010)?

Revisiting the site to ramp up for the 2019 class, I chanced upon
a post "Ramping Up: Dialogues on Feminism and Technology."[9] In
what proved to be my own 2013 blog post, I (re)read about what
we had done *then* to ramp up. I saw there a photo about this
reiterative practice of preparation. In its caption, I wrote: "Adrianne
Wadewitz schools some of the nodal instructors on feminist

interpretations of Wikipedia in my living room during our week-long summer prep meeting."

Adrianne died tragically about a year later while rock climbing. She had only recently been putting her body more fully into the world, only to fall tragically and violently out of it. She had been experimenting with a new kind of freedom with her fiancée after years of what she described as a more bookish and digital living. I include these words and images of her with his permission, and that of her parents. It seems useful to note here that Nishant's grandmother chose not to have her images used for similar purposes, and that Nishant's nephew is too young to be queried about consent.

This second digital gesture at a re-look of a lost interlocutor (the first was to Agnès Varda) serves as a reminder to remember and

[Figure 2.2]. Look again. Photograph: Alexandra Juhasz.

even feel, with some care, about one internet photo (and the
bubbly, smart, committed intellectual and person it captures).
This helps me to understand and emphasize that even if internet
time has changed drastically since I began that project only six
years ago, even if it runs by harsh standards and synchronizations,
I have the agency, need, and duty to honor and use my past work,
memories, and people as better suits me and them. If our dense
intertwined networked holdings of our recent, active, reflexive
digital thoughts seem *dated*—that is, stuck stupidly in the past and
not at all useful for the present; old-fashioned, out of date—this
need not be the role of *my* memory, writing, and all its attendant
personal data.

In their 2012 book *Cyberfeminism 2.0*—the first book we read
for the class, getting my students bristling because of its *dated*
terminology (and yet, they somehow failed to see how the exact
same concerns also started that book!)—Radhika Gajjala and Yeon
Ju On begin with Faith Wilding and Critical Art Ensemble's 1988 defi-
nition of cyberfeminim as "a promising new wave of thinking and
practice" (1). Gajjala and Oh continue: "Their persistent use of the
word 'Net,' now somehow archaic, reflects the vision of new media
technology for networking, that is, collective feminist theorizing
and practice" (1).

Archaic: "of a word or a style of language no longer in everyday use
but sometimes used to impart an old-fashioned flavor." Yuck . . .
"Net." The name for a once-cool place now cold, given that it is
frozen in time and peopled by the useless; not really the internet
we use now; they didn't have social media or apps; kinda really
fake, really! Networks populated by ghosts we can barely tolerate
listening to given that they have little to say of value and given
that their words are so weird. The dead or still alive, teaching
about the feminist internet (fine) but with the wrong terms or with
old-fashioned flavor (ick). The ghosts of ourselves listening (sad).
Our previous writing and projects endlessly hanging on well past
their prime.

Sarah Kember and Joanna Zylinska offer another feminist take on internet time, also the focus of their 2012 *Life after New Media*: "Maybe we want to feel like the internet dead are alive." Yes. Yes! "Mediation can be seen as another term for 'life,' for being-in and emerging-with the world" (23). The logic of the internet, one that fuels and is fueled by fakes (things, feelings, knowings) at an unprecedented and undifferentiable speed and volume, works by contriving and then inspiring us to feel that for our own energies to be the most potent, for us to be most alive (but always also exhausted), the recent past—and its glorious people and things—is and must be expendable. This is a computer-inspired fake. Nishant addresses many more examples of this in the stories he tells, ones where we are duped to not believe our own experiences of our own lives or where we dupe others to not see truths of ourselves. Stories of really fakes: when we choose to disrespect our own places, things, and times, often as a tactic of respect.

We can turn to cyberfeminism to counter such systems. For example, Wendy Chun wants us to seek "exhausting exhaustion; a recovery of the undead potential of our decisions and our information through a practice of constant care" (2016, 70). This I will understand as a cyberfeminist commitment to time, people, truth, and their technologies. This feminist time method must start with my own situated self. Myself as dated, present, and facing the future. My self reunited with yours. How might we inhabit multiple, co-present, co-influencing internet-ourselves? Let's start with looking at and like our selves.

Our memories run in and are mysterious illogical systems that are bigger than (even as they contain) space/time. Human storage: our bodies, too, hold memories. Our memories cannot hold everything, but they can embrace some of what we need at any given time. Given that the internet wants us to be in a perpetual present, what if we seek not distance (in space) but proximity (in time): that is connection; that is finding our truths as stored in space, and our bodies across and in time (and technology)? Backward, loving looks inspire radical futures.

3. Who Contrives the Moment?

Who contrives our internet moments? We can't really want to feel that the (so recently) dead are *dated*! Whose hubris underwrites and creates this bogus idea? Whose greed underwrites and creates this compelling need for the so-temporary internet now? Whose very real and controlling needs for the life and use of our data prevails? Whose very real and powerful needs make our data expendable, always flowing, allowing for such horrible damage to once-real people and to those of us who love them still? Nishant writes about computational logics and systems that overwrite our own attunements to where we live and how we do.

The ideas we created and their events, our methods and energies, the real time we had: these can be useful today, even if and because the internet changes at light speed. For technologies, humans, movements, and formats all work at different speeds, enjoy variant temporalities. Human lives are shorter than the movements we contribute to; books stay around and look and work pretty great across decades and centuries; web pages and their people look and talk antiquated (Emerson 2014). This aesthetic effect is rendered by out-of-style fonts and fashions. It intimates that what was rendered before is as old-fashioned as these forms, formats, and machines. But *that* is really fake. We should not buy into a design that expresses that "the human experience predicated on that data, and the biological body that is presumed to be mobile and outside of the computational network logic is suspicious, potentially subjective, indeterminate and fake."[10]

In her 2011, *Designing Culture: The Technological Imagination at Work,* Anne Balsamo sets forth terms similar to those used on Wikipedia to describe Adrianne's feminist work on Wikipedia. "Technoscience studies: to be analytically critical of the social and political consequences of the deployment of scientific knowledge, along with the technological logics and practices that emerge within scientific and technological institutions; and to be steadfastly supportive of, and encouraging to, the women who choose to pursue careers in these fields" (30–31).

[Figure 2.3]. As a major promoter of getting more women to edit Wikipedia to help end systematic bias, she [Adrianne Wadewitz] said, "We need more female editors, more feminists (who can be editors of any gender), and more editors willing to work on content related to women." Photograph: Alexandra Juhasz.

And, in their 2018 "Contrived Moment," a collective of queer feminist poets, writing together in Brighton, England, during one of my Fake News Poetry Workshops, also produce and model a local and time-stamped feminist technoscience at work.

Contrived moment

Something weird happened
To TIME
AT THE BACK
OF MY TONGUE
My body is the noise of
Everything I ever liked
Mutating like slime
mould
What if the mirror
Was our own
body? [11]

According to Wendy Chun, networks are "made out of time [memo-
ry and real time]" and some "threaten to take us out of time" (2016,
70). But our bodies, too, hold memory and real time. Our bodies
stay situated in time and place even if also scattered: *the noise of /
Everything I ever liked.* While each workshop has its own aims, the
one with the Devil's Dyke Collective was organized to listen to and
learn from that noise, itself contrived to keep us distracted and
slightly disoriented, *Mutating like slime / mould,* threatening to take
us out of time. Three collaborating teacher-poets (I always engage
with a poet from the place where we meet and make art together
about fake news), Linda Paoli, Claudia Treacher, and Helen Dixon,
created their workshop to "explore our presence on social media
and the contestation of fake/hegemonic news through creative
means" (fakenews-poetry.org). They organized the session using
somatic exercises speaking to feminist cyborg theory (Haraway
1991). They kept us focused in time and in our bodies, together
thinking and learning and feeling (about fakes).

Who contrives the moment? How was time made so weird? Many
forces brought us to this toxic internet and its speedy, irreverent
time. We talk, feel, and learn about just this in Fake News Poetry
Workshops where we listen to each other and also do some
internet research. (We spend some time in my #100hardtruths-
#fakenews primer on digital media literacy.) We make and take
time. We slow down and look at ideas, art, and history about fakes,
and then also at our real selves in our shared space: *What if the
mirror / Was our own / body?*

We study, understand, but seek not to replicate the technological
patriarchal logics and systems that are behind this immoral
mess. We follow Judy Wajcman, who spells out in *Technofeminism*
that "technology is a medium of power" (2004, 6). In that book's
Foreword, she relays how she updates her ten-year's earlier work,
Feminism Confronts Technology (1991). As is true for all who work in
critical internet studies, she strives to situate her effort temporally,
explaining that *something weird happened to time,* at least as far as
her work on the internet is concerned. Internet time accelerates

so quickly that it feels as if (our own) previous ideas need to be rewritten, or at least republished, just to remain the same.

It is really uncanny, weird, to write about a thing that changes faster than anything humans have previously known. Wendy Chun writes: "If analysis is interesting and definitive, it is too late: by the time we understand something, it has already disappeared or changed" (2016, 1). This creates a field-defining defensiveness: I write this now, even as I know it will be *dated* . . . immediately. "Media are reflexive historical subjects," Lisa Gitelman (2006, 20) explains in her entry in the genre, *Always Already New.* The internet is known for its speed *and* its reflexivity. There is a vast "tradition" of internet writing that names and works against and with its own datedness, including Chun's *Updating to Remain the Same: Habitual New Media,* and her work (2011, 2015) that led up to it. This particular time trouble—the internet's definitive speed, recursivity, and resulting *datedness*—haunts our scholarship, reflexively: as subject, content, and anxiety.

[Figure 2.4]. We reflect each other back. Photograph: Alexandra Juhasz.

It also fuels our fakes—*something weird happened / to TIME*—and can help focus a feminist response: What if the mirror was our own body?

4. Old-Fashioned Ways of Doing Things

> Adrianne Wadewitz was an American feminist scholar of 18th-century British literature, and a noted Wikipedian and commenter upon Wikipedia, particularly focusing on gender issues. In April 2014, Wadewitz died from head injuries from a fall while rock climbing.[12]

I met and began working with Adrianne Wadewitz in 2013—as is true for my coauthor Nishant Shah and series coeditor Wendy Chun—in our heady fertile years with FemTechNet. I still feel deeply connected and continue to benefit from these bygone associations: one way that I work to save myself. The past and its people are generative and can stay allied, if not alive. So, we save things that matter . . . for sustenance. The past and its people can be propagative forces if we use them well.

Stories of our previous encounters, how we date, remind us of fertile methods based in counterlogics and earlier times. Here's one: I cofounded this international collective with Anne Balsamo in the spring of 2013 in Los Angeles, California. Our manifold members have connected with the group for as many reasons as there are feminisms and technologies. Anne and I started FemTechNet for personal, professional, and political reasons. We wanted to build a network ("made out of time [memory and real time]" and their people). We did. We are. We move through and hold time with feminist technologies by way of explicit goals and their judiciously crafted methods; for instance, these from the longer list in FemTechNet's Manifesto:

> Accountability is a feminist technology.

> Collaboration is a feminist technology.

[Figure 2.5]. Adrianne Wadewitz and friends. Photograph: Alexandra Juhasz.

Collectivity is a feminist technology.

Care is a feminist technology.

Our cyberfeminism is first and foremost a principled and political technology. Our cyberfeminism is a means to more human and humane means. It is an activity: a process and method to better be with and know of real people, our world, and its (really fake) digital things. "We are an innovative learning technology."

To support (and save) ourselves, we built and build a network operating through feminist values and their supporting structures— accountability, collaboration, collectivity, care—one that is not as readily found elsewhere, one that counters the digital there and then. FemTechNet is a situated engagement with people and their things within a network made from *feminist internet time:* dated, placed, shared and shareable, remembered, felt, and connected. These are temporal and other connections that, contra the habitual digital, aren't built to "threaten to take us out of time" (Chun 2016, 70).

@FemTechNet we came and come together in real time, and linger
and last in its memories and technologies. These are methods to
save and use ourselves differently from the patriarchal, corporate,
weaponized internet. We better our internet lot by saving, doing,
and collectively working toward a something else that we are eager
to name: specific things that can be better for women (cis and
trans), people, and our technologies. We start from an informed
ethical tradition and connect to collective inspiration (Wernimont
2019; McPherson 2018). We are not alone. "FemTechNet is distributed expertise. FemTechNet is an experiment in solidarity."

In 2012, still real-life strangers but already longtime intellectual
allies, Anne and I met for the first time to discuss over lunch our
mutual interests in AIDS and the media. We quickly learned another vital connection. We had both recently released significant and
innovative ventures into critical internet studies: my born-digital
"video-book" about YouTube with MIT (2011), Anne's "transmediat-
ed book" (2011) about technological design and imagination with
Duke. We promptly discovered another link: how we were both
smarting alone, worried that our works had been minimized or
mis-seen by critical internet and media studies due to our overt
feminist politics and/or related creative or innovative formats or
methods. How affirming then to find each other, name a shared
professional letdown, and understand our experiences as systematic and not merely personal (Redstockings 1979; Sarachild 1978)!
We understood that such blocks on learning from and knowing
each other—forcefully introduced through structured network
disconnection—were critical conditions of the contemporary
internet (scholarly) culture we sought to understand and better,
just as they had been and are true of patriarchy.

So, there and then over lunch, we committed to a project to save
ourselves. We would locate, organize, and activate our legitimate
and interested peers and interlocutors: those working on technology through a feminist lens, those who were also largely (and
systemically) separated or mis-seen due to scattered disciplines,
occupations, places of origin, and a field-defining misogyny with its

lingering mistrust of feminism or disdain for feminists. We hoped that in so doing, feminist technology studies would become more visible, better visibilized, and thus accessible and useful in its diversity and complexity, as well as better networked globally to past and present iterations. As *dated* as this may now seem given the hypervisibility of "popular feminism" online (Banet-Wesier 2018), there was a time, 2013, when our project was urgent.

Just as it is today. Feminist digital methods allow us to use internet things in our own alternative networked internet time: saving ourselves differently from the corporate internet's perpetual viral movement. On the corporate internet "what gets circulated is not anchored onto bodies and spaces."[13] It is easily fueled by deceit, disdain, patriarchal violence, and necessary procedures and feelings of expendability, obsolescence, and fakery (Fitzpatrick 2011). As a collective, we would mark the terrain of what we do and know, what we feminists did and learned of and with technology, time, authenticity, and power, and as critically, how all this continues to be done back at us. Contra misogyny, we became the author, audience, mentor, instigator, critic, developer, user, and catalyst each one of us and many, many more needed. "FemTechNet is a power tool" (FemTechNet Manifesto).

Feel free to read about and also see, saved and repeated, one record of our earliest collective efforts in a blog post[14] and its image of Adrianne Wadewitz and many others in 2013, meeting for the first time at our inaugural summer working group, "Ramping Up: Dialogues on Feminism and Technology." As had been true for Anne and me, and as was definitive for feminists working in technology at that moment, few of us had actually met before twenty or so strangers showed up, unfunded and highly curious, at my house and online, from all over the country and the world, for a driven week of intoxicating creation and dedicated interaction.

By so countering the definitive structure of datedness built into today's internet experience, aesthetics, storage, and use, we see avenues of thinking and practice that form one up-to-date

response to the current crisis of fake news. Old-fashioned cyberfeminist frameworks are useful traditions to better save ourselves.

5. Making Data Precious

We can experience *datedness* (a thing, person, or event from the
past, now timestamped, blogrolled [Dean 2010; Lovink 2007], and
stuck there for [the] good with so much more accumulated around
and on top) as *precious.* Helpful. Valuable. Good. Not in the sense
of monetary worth, but in any saved thing's immeasurable capacities for use, action. I want to be clear. Most of the things we were
fighting for and feeling then are still here, maybe worse and only
sometimes better or even over. When you date (and place something), that inscription marks that it was once in a place and in real
time (online, in a room, no matter) and that matters: regardless of
changes in words, gizmos, or the just right haircut.

While going on *dates* can be fun and sexy, *datedness* is neither, at
least as it is currently contrived for us. But what if we thought of
datedness like a date between people in their time and ours: a
situated feminist model for hooking up and networking in time.
Feminist datedness is useful for all moral citizens interested in
thinking differently about fakes (and other things) on the internet.
Feminist internet time begins with connection—through memory,
photographs, stories, poems—to the specificity of being, doing, and
intelligence—the many truths of any situated bodily experience
rendered returnable through records of its data.

While *things* can certainly be *dated*—past their sell-by date, a
perishable product that might make you ill or kill you—methods,
processes, goals, and their peoples should and cannot be held to
this metric. Methods, processes, goals, and people are gloriously
ineffable, unstable, unstampable, responsive. These stay useful
even when their once real time is over. We stamp them not to
keep them stuck but to indicate that they once were real, there
and then, just like that, in all their capacious possibility. Feminist
processes can cherish and use *dated* things that were once

connected to ourselves in real time. Our cyberfeminist processes are goal oriented, mobile, useful, and should not be immediately rendered inoperable or obsolescent by corporate mandate (Philip and DaCosta 2010; Consalvo and Passonen 2002). Memory as human process. Chun here: "Memory is an action, an activation and difference in structure, making memory not anything because it is everything" (2016, 89).

Poetry as human process: one method to slow down, to see, honor, and engage with our past as precious; an activation, a feminist process; a live way to engage or enliven dead things. What if to timestamp didn't mean to shelve but to activate, move differently, and in this way . . . escape?

Moving

St. Louis was my sunrise.
The horizon and I by ourselves.
I met my match mid-twirl.
For a moment, time stood still in Central Park.
Puerto Rico, where life's greatest gift was given
and taken too soon.
We built our life in Brooklyn.
Now I live alone.
My existence remains for others.

—Nina Daro, Mahalia Hughes-Roussel, and Allison Rapp, 2019 Fake News Poetry Workshop at Brooklyn College[15]

Our existence remains for others. Make the *dated* precious as a form of saying and doing I love you and also myself.

6. Moving in/out of Storage

Our feminist internet goals, methods, and their scholarly traditions can stay useful and truthful (even as they adapt), even as the internet and other technologies change, if we can engage with stamina, that is with strength over time, together.

[Figure 2.6]. Our dead are precious. Photograph: Alexandra Juhasz.

How do we best make fun of power?

radical
change
cannot
come from
isolation;
it must be
collaborative
....
time
+
repetition
+
stamina
in material

—Couplet of fragments produced at
Toronto FNPW, 2018[16]

32   *Stamina / in material.* Dare scratch below the surface of the internet. Touch its messy myriad materials—time and repetition and collaboration. Discover that much of this remains, well, utterly pertinent, not yet attended to, used up, or finished. The past is not immaterial but just in material. See beyond how the words, websites, and ways of the internet past feel as obsolete as the ever-changing jargon we need to keep up with its hustle. Save not to update but to cherish and use.

Locate, understand, and rejoice in the fact of our ongoing situated-ness in internet (and real) space and time. This is a feminist cyber-method of validation—of self, truth, community, and knowledge. It counters machinic techniques of indexicality, legalistic processes of evidence, governmental systems of status, corporate systems of popularity, and other patriarchal and powerful systems of digital verification responsible for making the internet the really fake that it has become (Collins 1990; Harding 2015). "We need to demystify the internet by viewing it as material and situated," explain Ramesh Srinivasan and Adam Fish in their *After the Internet* (2017, 13). Theirs is another work of internet scholarship that challenges the use of temporal frameworks by suggesting place-based work, the "provincializing [of] our understandings, or seeing them within the matrices of culture, context, and politics" (21).

They suggest nothing new. We relish something old-fashioned, like saying to my kids, "no phones at the dinner table." Let's begin again and attend differently to and with internet time as provincialized. We can start by slowing down to see whence our shared saved past sits . . .

So . . . . let's actually *look* at the photo of Adrianne: and all that was really there in my living room, just as it really is no longer. "The information is always up for grabs and subject to interpretations where her own meanings give these pictures life."[17]

[. . . . .]

Adrianne. Pictured in a snapshot in my living room on the huge red antique carpet that I burned with a stray ember from my once-family's beloved fireplace—not caught in this frame but opening out directly in front of Adrianne—creating a hole that I lied about, always, to my ex-husband (I don't know *how* that happened! Really fake). Adrianne, surrounded by and so well teaching the strangers who would become friends, hers and mine . . .

An animated body caught on camera moving with exuberance and also, perhaps, gentle tentativeness. Adrianne and a handful of others pictured in the living room of the home I once shared with my ex-husband and then-teenage children in the city I used to live, Los Angeles. Ramesh visited us there once. We sat around the outside fire pit and told stories. Adrienne lived in my neighborhood. She came to Claremont to make videos for FemTechNet. We

[Figure 2.7]. Summer 2013, Los Angeles. Photograph: Alexandra Juhasz.

were wowed by, and wanted to record and share, all that she knew. She is caught teaching us about Wikipedia from a feminist lens, and how to work it better for feminists.

Adrianne, in a sleeveless summer shirt. Ginger hair short. Glasses. Funny. *Nerdy.* Warm. Amazingly enthusiastic and knowledgeable about something that seemed so wonky and strange then: getting women onto Wikipedia. Today, *everyone* knows how important such efforts are. How *dated.* (Some things are *dated* because they are improved or are at least getting done.[18])

. . . .

her body turned to include all the listeners in the room, some, like the fireplace, fire pit, and carpet burn offscreen. Our bodies aimed at hers. Attentive. We are learning together and meeting each other. It looks intense, warm, and real. It was. And that's what I see. I was there. And I remember. My body, too, holds time and memory. I will not be distracted.

do not be distracted from the truth

do not be distracted from the truth
that you make with your own body.
solidity is a useful illusion,
it gets us through the day.
but solidity dupes us.
tectonic assurance is fragile ground.
the truth is in the way we move
the truth is in the impressionability of us,
the truth is a space we fight to shape.

—M. Astley, at a Fake News Poetry Workshop in
Brighton England, 2018[19]

I chanced upon this photo online. The picture, like networks, like me, holds many truths about itself, as well as about time and memory. When I saw it again, anew, I enjoyed that rare and momentary shock of the new. That punctum that even an internet image (really fake as they can be; voluminous and less-powerful as they've all

become) can sometimes hold. I saw it again and felt some sort of
reverse of what mostly happens when we chance upon the internet
of 2013: things, encounters, meetings, and their websites, words,
and ways that just don't look and sound right, like now, or like the
truth. Like how Facebook surprises us with a photo of ourselves
from a year ago, or five. Nishant tells me that some people have
been traumatized by these unexpected blasts from the past,
returns initiated by an algorithm just because they held that year's
highest count of likes. But sometimes three-years-ago's biggest hit
was an image of a tragedy, a death, an ex-boyfriend, a lost friend.
Our dated data needs care in its selection, sharing, (re)circulation,
and use, if we hope to connect to, remember, and value its many
truths.

Chun writes: "What is real unfolds in 'real time.' If earlier visual
indexicality guaranteed authenticity (a photograph was real
because it indexed something out there), now 'real time' does so,
for 'real time' points elsewhere, to 'real-world' events, to the user's
captioned actions. That is 'real time' introduced indexicality to this
seemingly anti-indexical medium" (2016, 75). Real time: so *dated.*
Yes. Yes!

7. Perched on Indeterminacy

In my earlier, more optimistic writing about "productive fakes" and
their filmic practices written after producing the first African American lesbian feature film, a rather famous case of a fake documentary, *The Watermelon Woman* (Cheryl Dunye, 1996), I was interested
in techniques that could create distance between audience and
text, between text and formal tradition (Juhasz and Lerner 2006).
This spatial metaphor and related tactics evince how faking, as a
representational approach (and in the right context), can allow for
a perceiving subject's critical difference from the commonsense
logic of a thing.

But as fake media and fake news become ever more dominant,
as its contexts and conditions change, I began to see, particularly

online, on YouTube, this same tactic being used for different ends and audiences (2011). Faking not for distance. Faking as a means toward distortion enabled by the too proximate. I changed my mind as the fake media changed me, the real media, and the world. I began to believe that in this context—social media, internet President—fakeness stopped clarifying. In this time and place, in this internet, fakeness muddled meaning and values. Faking's goals transformed into seeding confusion and disorientation. Faking instigated a disavowal of the real and our beliefs in it. "The indeterminate human will be forced into determinate meanings through computation logics."[20]

Given today's vast reach, powers, and corporations of computation, I do and think something else with and about fakes. I work to enact some human tactics and forms in the face of fake news. I seek for systems of indeterminacy and internal contradiction that we can hold as true, by making good use of poetry, not internet video.

Let me be very clear here. Tactics are contingent; forms are tactics. To manifest and study contingency can lead to clarity and complexity, or it can produce muddle. Formats are ideology free and context dependent. Tactics and forms are there to be used and taken, they are expendable, they are useful. Until they aren't. But we feminists have ongoing commitments. This is why we seek and also break forms as tactics. I am an activist and a teacher, a concerned citizen and artist, and my explicit goals are and have been consistent across the recent past of twenty-five years or so: to use technology and art forms to engage with others to better understand and then behave differently from the corporate media, including the internet. I must make a move. If fakes are toxic, we can seek other methods to understand, combat, and gain power. When fakes free us, we use them with aplomb.

8. Virality Is Virility

For today, fakes are violent and misogynist. A potent mix of internet-fueled falsity, masculine grandiosity, and resulting real-

world bellicosity undergird fake news and our efforts to understand it. The internet seeks, supports, and succeeds via virality,
which is understood as a truism and a good, as self-evidently
powerful and right, as the truest pursuit of the habitat. This is
really fake. Virality is a precondition for fake news (Juhasz 2017).
When ideas move fast—in their production, reception, or pass-
along—we give up the time necessary for research, verification,
contemplation, and action. #fakenews—unlike real news—reveals
the logic and cycles of virality, a mad explosion of attention that
flattens and simplifies whatever is under scrutiny by having to bear,
while needing to use, the weight of mass attention and production. "Competing truth claims are verified and legitimized though
the systems of power that parse them."[21] All the good work that
happens in response becomes ever harder to see given the clamor
and the clutter, the too many manipulative misuses and steady
sarcastic re-renders muddling our vision. Exhaustion. A gutting of
integrity. A quick hard move to deception, irony, play. Then, watch
out: the confusing, bizarre reversal of the thing itself (fake becomes
real and then back again). This is made particularly baffling when
the viral subject is itself *fakeness* (Young 2019). The real story now
seems as superficial or at least ironic as the frenzy it began. Bore-
dom, disinterest, jokes, lolz are left in its wake: "What is at stake in
this irony is not simply satire that presents itself as such, but rather
the collapse of a vantage point for adjudicating between satire and
sincerity" (Young 2019).

Virality is good for branding, selling, fun, and power. But virality,
not so great for social justice and our cyberfeminism with which we
work for it. We need depth, connection, careful consideration, and
usability over brief recognition, superficial attention, or momentary
if strong emotion. "Outlast virility," I suggest, in relation to a cycle
of news, #fakenews, and related actions that have accelerated to
a dangerous pitch where rational, legal, and ethical care and consideration can no longer be exacted before we act. "Outlast virility"
in connection to said speed and the virile weaponized powers of
patriarchal aggression it authorizes.

Technology can be used for good and bad things.
It can be used for creating and destroying.
We can use technology for making our lives
    more convenient.
It can also be used as a means of protection
    from evil.
Each instrument is used for a specific purpose.
It can also be used for committing and
    preventing crimes.
If technology is used in a bad way it can destroy
    the world.
We need to prevent that from happening.
We need technology so that good can triumph
    over evil.

—Harvey P, made at a Fake News Poetry Workshop
at Poets of Course, New York City, 2019[22]

Each instrument is used for a specific purpose. As internet fakery results in ever more real-world bellicosity, as violence moves from representation to lived space, I begin to doubt that our decades of work on digital media literacy can be useful for today's instrument of violence. In these conditions, I doubt previous tactics. And that's how I get to poetry, and to Harvey P. At Fake News Poetry Workshops individuals' truths about fakes are rendered as place-based, interactive research through talking, listening, and art making about #fakenews. *Technology can be used for good and bad things.*

9. Fakeness Can Be Unstuck

Fakes are things. Sometimes we create them as "conditions of ethical behavior." This is what I once wrote about. In the 1990s and even earlier, I thought that fake documentary could be a method of saving ourselves in feminist queer time. In 2009, I was invited to contribute to a special issue of *No More Potlucks* about copies. As a producer and actor in *The Watermelon Woman* and editor of a

related scholarly book, *F is for Phony: Fake Documentary and Truth's* **39**
Undoing (Juhasz and Lerner 2006), I was a champion of the queer
productive fake.

But, by 2009 that work was *dated.* My scholarly and activist media
praxis had moved to the internet. My work with fakes had been
shaken by the communicative norms of this technology and its
time. In this lengthy excerpt from "The Increasingly Unproductive
Fake," you can see me try to map how my thinking and use of fakes
moves through time:

Dunye establishes that identity and history, the stuff of life
and its images, becomes most authentic and empowering
when mediated through technologies of preservation and
display. In *The Watermelon Woman,* black lesbian (film)
history and identity are simultaneously embedded in and
distanced from disciplinary systems like a mainstream
body of texts and textual practices that ignore or create
them, and this particular film, *The Watermelon Woman,*
that records and shows fake images of black lesbians'
all-too-real experience. To do so, Dunye and Cheryl must
mimic and at the same time mine the tools, institutions,
forms, and technologies of history making. She mocks and
also assumes the position of one authorized to remember, represent, and have history. Unmaking (and taking
up) documentary authority allows Dunye to unmask
institutionally sanctioned disremembering in the form of
protective archivists who disallow Cheryl access to their
records, misogynist collectors uninterested in unearthing
documents by women, or black community members who
forget their forays with whites. And yet the result in *The
Watermelon Woman* is not a morass of misinformation,
with identity and history left undone and unmade. Marlon
Fuentes reminds us that the gaps and ellipses of history
are "just as important as the objects we have in our
hands." The intangible is not inarticulate: it speaks in an
unauthorized, untranslated tongue understood by some.

In *The Watermelon Woman,* Fae speaks to Cheryl in a voice both expressive and inconclusive. And Cheryl can hear her. This is enough to empower Cheryl, at film's end, to conclude, "I *am* a black lesbian filmmaker and I have a lot to say." She learns a truth that she needs from the lie that she made which is Fa(k)e.

Dunye and Cheryl's simultaneous avowal and disavowal of the real marks *The Watermelon Woman* as a productive fake. An (unstable) identity is created, a community (of skeptics) is built, and an (unresolved) political statement about black lesbian history and identity is articulated. The desire to say and hear something true through words and images that are fragmentary and even fake is the multiple project of the productive fake documentary.

For the purposes of this contribution to *No More Potlucks,* I could easily re-name such self-aware faking (or copying) a queering strategy (really, no potlucks, *ever?*! you're not serious, are you? They're actually kinda fun, and it's the only place left to get a good devilled egg!) The queer copy marks and thus unsettles binaries of stable being, knowing, and showing and inserts a question, joke, or angry exclamation where once only certainty held firm.

In much more recent writing (Juhasz, "Even Obama"), I argue that the language of fake documentary has become the dominant vernacular of YouTube, and therefore, this once queer strategy has become toothless, or unqueer, or straight. Whatever. The ironic wedge, sometimes also known as camp, which long and well served the underserved of the modern and post-modern by allowing for a critique of the norm by using its very discourses of power against it, is now the discourse of power.

Fakes are verified and mobilized, useful and violent, depending on their times and technologies. Fakes are a matter of style, law, profit, and power. They become easily *dated,* and then not particularly useful. Fakeness and faking are operations that occur within cultural contexts where understandings of authenticity, and the power that accrues to the real and the fake, are always changing. Look again at the photo of Adrianne that I have shown you six times. The pixels, color, and detail of the camera lock her into an already lost digital stylistic. "If truthful media objects carry with them the potential instability and uncertainty of being otherwise, the same affordance needs to be granted to fakeness."[23]

As a scholar and maker of fake media, as a friend and colleague of real people, I read and share (and try to be caring toward) ghosts of myself, and others, who grapple with the relation between (fake) media and social justice. We have worked, as Nishant and I do here, to better understand how really fake things can both harm and empower activists and their movements. Across media, movements, and time, I argue that fakes depend on how they are used, who makes them, and for what purpose. The power of any one thing's fakeness is not stuck. Fakes can be unstuck with methods of care.

10. Individual Truths–Collective Fakes

for we understood their suffering, didn't we?

Prompt: meditate upon a line from Jennifer Moxley's Clampdown (2009), ". . . for we / understood their suffering, didn't we, and we / were the ones who took it upon ourselves to make it new."

We were the ones who took it upon ourselves to make it new. The time of modernism (vintage new) vs. the time of the event (actually new?) vs. the time of suffering (keep it underspecified). A new poem has the most current timestamp, though these can be forged, and the time bars scrubbed. A new poetry is exciting (desublimation) and can be explained quickly in an elevator.

—Kyle Booten[24]

42 Kyle Booten practices feminist technoscience at work . . . . as poetry. He shared this poem after the first Fake News Poetry Workshop in January 2018, where he was the larger project's first workshop facilitator. Held at the Ammerman Center's Biennial Symposium on Art and Technology, Kyle designed a workshop where writing poems together about fake news would be "a chance to work through what it would mean to use poetic forms explicitly as psychotechnologies of care, algorithms of attention that could possibly restructure consciousness in ways that run counter to those enforced by the programming industries" (Booten 2018).

Who contrived the moment? *We were the ones who took it upon ourselves to make it new.* The time of suffering (and its related caring) is outside of time (Scary 1987). Like networks, or fakes, suffering can take us out of time. Suffering is time compounded and time too big to bear or explain. And yet we do. We can learn from time and its suffering, try to remember and share it. Date it. *A new poem has the most current timestamp, though these can be forged, and the time bars scrubbed.* But the body knows. The time of suffering is not easy to capture in a photo with its cruel, stupid, indifferent, machinic, and forgeable timestamp.

But some of the authenticity of suffering can, and has for centuries, been rendered, saved, and shared via another truth-telling medium (*desublimation:* from one state to another with no intermediate liquid stage): poetry.

11. It Is Not Fake If It Fools You

Fake News Poetry Workshops have taught me about humans' capacity and yearning to know and be well.[25] At workshops, people together listen and also put into words their interpretations and feelings about truth and deception, reality and representation, social media and sociality. Humans want to and can learn in and across time through cyberfeminist methods of accountability, collaboration, collectivity, and care; this is harder to do in the internet; this is very much about the internet.

Much current digital media literacy tries to arm us to deduce and confirm (and thus defuse) fakes through fact-finding, authenticating, and verification. These skills are undoubtedly part of a worthy response, if not a solution. However, these tactics are of and stay rooted in the corruption that got us here in the first place. "Circulation is the digital currency, and information that cannot travel is never going to attain truth value."[26] The free-floating, unverified trash on the internet is one person's weapon and another's truth. But if the truths we render in response are partial, personal, and of their own place and time, they need never be substantiated. Can we create and engage in practices that perform, as per Chun, "a recovery of the undead potential of our decisions and our information through a practice of constant care" (2016, 70).

Poems can be carefully and caringly expressed, listened to, and shared. Poems can be rendered again as something connected and new but not viral, in that the sharing is slow, considered, and of its place and time.

> Fake News Poetry Workshops are interested in and contra the logics of the internet that have flamed fake news into the fire it is today. *Easy* is not one of its beliefs or operating structures. This is also true of quick, anonymous, viral, mean, profit-driven, memetic, on indexical. That is to say, Fake News Poetry Workshops are one way to counter those internet modes and values; the corrupt ways of being and knowing that use the internet and social media to create, move, fuel, and weaponize fake news.
>
> Making poetry together with people about fake news works: in the valuable things it makes and more so, by highlighting other ethical, communal, feminist processes of doing and knowing. The project has verified for me some good news in the face of fake news. We can gather together through other structures, in our many local places, to generate, hold, and share some "art answers to fake questions."

. . . Enjoy! I know these poems hold wisdom and beauty from which we can begin to encounter and counter the structuring logics of fake news. And I believe that art-making, connected to our articulated experiences of self, community, place, and truth, then rendered as poetry, can be one small part of a shared way out of, or perhaps around about, our terrible troubles. However, no news is good news. The poems written at FNPWs do not offer nor are they solutions, just an invitation and an invocation to act and do a little differently for the better of the internet and ourselves (Juhasz 2020).

Indeterminacy is a human capacity that lets more than one truth comingle on any page or in any body: the past and present, dread and hope, one memory that becomes many, each different, all true.

12. Life ≠ Spectacle

As I first write this in January 2019 (and then edit again in November in Hawaii!), I am in Pasadena, although my home is now in New York. I walk the blocks of the streets where I once lived and also walked, pushing my babies, and then strolling or biking with kids and later still adolescents (time measured by their change and growth and movement). We were together taking the air, loosening up, over twenty-one years. I've been gone for three. When I'm in New York, sure, I remember LA. I look at pictures. I dig deep into my own interior and recall. But memory is an action, in action. When I walk these streets, what pours back, rolls in, is monumentally full, extreme, intense, beautiful, mine. Not *dated* in the least but dateful. Full! Exhausting and rich in its layers and colors. Its temporal density caught in space. Each house. The details! I remember them all. The trees and vistas.

This space is my blood and heart so open-ended but finite. The space is the street, the block, the neighborhood that holds and loosens memories held in me. This is where I lived. I am always now and then locked onto the streets of what will always be my neighborhood, at least for as long as I live. So parochial. So real.

Places hold time, as memories and real time, unleashed for us by our bodies that also hold memories and real time, by moving through it. Given that our bodies too are a network—physically and mentally rewarded and activated by smells, colors, lived details, and air—a situated cyberfeminist analysis of fakes can use poetry as a vehicle, receptacle, excuse, and method to engage our bodies, in their own time and place, and authenticate a truth from another real time, one that can be connected to and used by others.

No matter the promise or lie of social media, real life is ordinary and everyday. *Forget THE AUDIENCE,* you never had one really. They

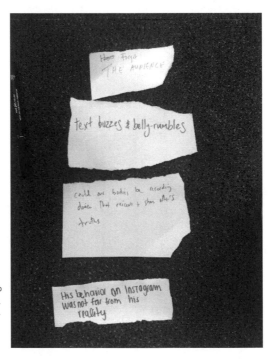

[Figure 2.8]. Photo of poetry process. Photograph: Alexandra Juhasz.

were really fake. Contrived by and for you to make time weird. *His behaviour on Instagram / was not far from his / reality.* But the people we know and knew, they were and are real.

Networks are made of and hold time and memory. Let go of the structures and feelings of *datedness* as a corporate and controlling logic of a perpetual now, one responsible for repeatable contrived moments that serve to disconnect us from our own recent past, and its very real people, so as to sell us things, lies, and violence in its place. Instead, poetry can release us to work and think differently within and about networked time and its resultant fakes.

The corporate internet holds and uses time for bad ends: to build up evermore fakes that sever us from our past, each other, and the truth. But lived space, our connected bodies, social movements, and poetry are also networks for time that can keep us truthful. *Text buzzes & belly-rumbles.* Feminist internet time is dated, placed, shared and shareable, remembered, felt, and connected. There and then we engage in caring, connected, ethical, and thoughtful practices of verification in known places and time-stamped moments. The vehicle for these holdings shifts from indexical media (film, photo, video) to poetry as a *dated* and up-to-date form of validation. *Could our bodies be the recording devices that receive and share others' truths?*

Notes

1   In this effort, I will map many related attempts (by feminists, postcolonial, queer, trans, or antiracist scholars) to press against, be companion to, or interrupt the methods and interests of the digital humanities or critical internet studies writ large.

2   This essay maps cyberfeminist theory and practice alongside digital fakes, problems with time, and poetry. It is not an introduction to cyberfeminism, but I am eager to use references as one method to introduce readers to this rich, unfolding, lengthy, lively, and lovely body of thought. Many of the authors I will cite are my fellow members of FemTechNet, a distributed network of feminists working on technology who model many of this effort's understandings of space, time, collectivity, and care. But, as I will say in the essay, this tradition began earlier. So to begin: "the bitch mutant manifesto" (VNS Matrix 1996):

"Sucked in, down through a vortex of banality. You have just missed the twentieth century. You are on the brink of the millennium—which one—what does it
matter?" For more about VNX Matrix and the dawn of cyberfeminism, see The
Old Boys Network: https://www.obn.org.

3   http://scalar.usc.edu/nehvectors/100hardtruths-fakenews/index.

4   http://scalar.usc.edu/nehvectors/100hardtruths-fakenews/fake-news-r-us.

5   http://scalar.usc.edu/nehvectors/100hardtruths-fakenews/37-size-matters-we
    -have-to-be-minimalist.

6   http://fakenews-poetry.org/poems/docbc.html.This and all poems following can
    be found online, in differing contexts, at #100HardTruths-#FakeNews: http://
    scalar.usc.edu/nehvectors/100hardtruths-fakenews/index or at fakenews
    -poetry.org. Or on paper in *My Phone Lies to Me: Fake News Poetry Workshops as
    Radical Digital Media Literacy* (manuscript, Juhasz).

7   Nishant Shah, "Between Memory and Storage: Real Approaches to Fakeness,"
    this volume, in the section, "Virality Is Virility."

8   Nishant Shah, "Between Memory and Storage," this volume, in the section
    "Moving In/Out of Storage."

9   http://www.feministonlinespaces.com/2013/08/ramping-up-dialogues-on
    -feminism-and-technology.

10 Nishant Shah, "Between Memory and Storage," this volume, in the section
    "Virality Is Virility."

11 http://fakenews-poetry.org/dd-list.html.

12 Wikipedia, "Adrianne Wadewitz."

13 Nishant Shah, "Between Memory and Storage," this volume, in the section
    "Virality Is Virility."

14 http://www.feministonlinespaces.com/2013/08/ramping-up-dialogues-on
    -feminism-and-technology.

15 http://fakenews-poetry.org/docbc-list.html.

16 http://fakenews-poetry.org/toronto-list.html.

17 Nishant Shah, "Between Memory and Storage," this volume, in the section "Life
    ≠ Spectacle."

18 See more about FemTechNet's Wikistorming efforts and methods: http://
    femtechnet.org/docc/feminist-wiki-storming or at our sister org art+feminism:
    http://www.artandfeminism.org.

19 http://fakenews-poetry.org/poems/brighton.html.

20 Nishant Shah, "Between Memory and Storage," this volume, in the section
    "Perched on Indeterminacy."

21 Nishant Shah, "Between Memory and Storage," this volume, in the section
    "Perched on Indeterminacy."

22 http://fakenews-poetry.org/poems/cathy.html.

23 Nishant Shah, "Between Memory and Storage," this volume, in the section
    "Fakeness Can Be Unstuck."

24 http://fakenews-poetry.org/ammerman-list.html.

25 The idea that "it is not fake if it fools you" is developed in the "Introduction" to
    F is for Phony (Juhasz and Lerner 2006).

26 Nishant Shah, "Between Memory and Storage," this volume, in the section
"Virality Is Virility."

References

Ahmed, Sara. 2016. *Living a Feminist Life.* Durham, N.C.: Duke University Press.

Balsamo, Anne. 2011. *Designing Culture:* The Technological Imagination at Work.
Durham, N.C.: Duke University Press.

Barad, Karen. 2007. *Meeting the Universe Halfway: Quantum Physics and the Entanglement of Matter and Meaning.* Durham, N.C.: Duke University Press.

Banet-Weiser, Sarah. 2018. *Empowered.* Durham, N.C.: Duke University Press.

Booten, Kyle. 2018. "Psychotechnologies of Care." https://medium.com/the-operating
-system/10-tries-100-poems-take-1-field-notes-psychotechnologies-of-care-algo
rithms-of-attention-db48f6a3043d.

boyd, danah. 2017. "Did Media Literacy Backfire?" January 5. https://points.datasoci
ety.net/did-media-literacy-backfire-7418c084d88d.

Braidotti, Rosi. 2012. *Nomadic Theory.* New York: Columbia University Press.

Cardenas, Micha. 2012. *The Transreal: Political Aesthetics of Crossing Realities.* New
York: Atropos Press.

Carpio, Genevieve. 2019. *Collisions at the Crossroads: How Place and Mobility Make
Race.* Berkeley: University of California Press.

Chun, Wendy. 2011. *Programmed Visions.* Cambridge, Mass.: MIT Press.

Chun, Wendy. 2016. *Updating to Remain the Same: Habitual New Media* Cambridge,
Mass: MIT Press.

Chun, Wendy, ed. 2015. *New Media, Old Media,* 2d ed. New York: Routledge.

Coleman, Beth. 2011. *Hello Avatar.* Cambridge, Mass: MIT Press.

Collins, Patricia Hill. 1990. *Black Feminist Thought.* Boston: Unwin Hyman Press.

Consalvo, Mia, and Susanna Paasonen. 2002. *Women & Everyday Uses of the Internet.*
New York: Peter Lang Publishing.

Daniels, Jesse. 2009. "Rethinking Cyberfeminism(s): Race, Gender, and Embodiment,"
Women's Studies Quarterly 37 1–2 (Spring/Summer): 101–24.

Dean, Jodi. 2010. *Blog Theory: Feedback and Capture in the Circuits of Drive.* New York:
Polity Press.

Emerson, Lori. 2014. *Reading Writing Interfaces.* Minneapolis: University of Minnesota
Press.

FemTechNet. n.d. Center for Solutions to Online Violence. https://femtechnet.org/
csov.

FemTechNet. n.d. Manifesto. https://femtechnet.org/publications/manifesto.

Fernández, Maria. 2002. "Is Cyberfeminism Colorblind?" http://www.artwomen.org/
cyberfems/fernandez/fernandez1.htm.

Fitzpatrick, Kathleen. 2011. *Planned Obsolescence.* New York: New York University
Press.

Fotopoulou, Aristea, Alexandra Juhasz, and Kate O'Riordan, eds. 2014. *Ada 5: Queer
Feminist Media Praxis.* https://adanewmedia.org/issues/issue-archives/issue5/.

Gajjala, Radhika. 2019. *Digital Diasporas: Labor and Affect in Gendered Indian Digital Publics.* Lanham, Md.: Rowman & Littlefield International.

Gajjala, Radhika, and Yeon Ju Oh. 2012. eds. *Cyberfeminism 2.0.* New York: Peter Lang).

Giannachi, Gabriella. 2016. *Archive Everything: Mapping the Everyday.* Cambridge, Mass.: MIT Press.

Gitelman, Lisa. 2006. *Always Already New.* Cambridge, Mass.: MIT Press.

Gordon, Eric, and Paul Mihailidis. 2016. *Civic Media.* Cambridge, Mass.: MIT Press.

Gray, Mary. 2010. *Out in the Country: Youth, Media, and Queer Visibility in Rural America.* New York: New York University Press.

Haraway, Donna. 1991. "A Cyborg Manifesto: Science, Technology, and Socialist Feminism in the Late Twentieth Century." In *Simians, Cyborgs and Women: The Reinvention of Nature,* 149–81. New York: Routledge.

Harding, Sandra. 2015. *Objectivity and Diversity: Another Logic of Scientific Research.* Chicago: University of Chicago Press.

Harpold, Terry, and Kavita Philip, eds, 2010. *Going Native: Cyberculture and Postcolonialism.* New York: Routledge.

Juhasz, Alexandra. 2009. "Even Obama: Irony in the Time of YouTube." January 16. https://aljean.wordpress.com/2009/01/16/even-obama-irony-in-the-time-of-youtube.

Juhasz, Alexandra. 2009. "The Increasingly Unproductive Fake." *no more potlucks* 4 (July–August). http://nomorepotlucks.org/site/the-increasingly-unproductive-fake.

Juhasz, Alexandra. 2011. *Learning from YouTube.* Cambridge, Mass.: MIT Press. http://vectors.usc.edu/projects/learningfromyoutube.

Juhasz, Alexandra. 2017. "Trump's Ultra Male Posturing Was Made for Our Media Age." *Dame Magazine,* September 7. https://www.damemagazine.com/author/alexandra-juhasz.

Juhasz, Alexandra. 2020. "My Phone Lies to Me: Fake News Poetry Workshops as Radical Digital Media Literacy." Unpublished manuscript.

Juhasz, Alexandra. n.d. "#100HardTruths-#FakeNews." http://scalar.usc.edu/neh vectors/100hardtruths-fakenews/index.

Juhasz, Alexandra. n.d. Fake News Poetry Workshops. fakenews-poetry.com.

Juhasz, Alexandra. n.d. Feminist Online Spaces. http://www.feministonlinespaces.com.

Juhasz, Alexandra. n.d. We Need Gentle Truths for Now. https://shows.acast.com/we-need-gentle-truths-for-now/.

Juhasz, Alexandra, and Jesse Lerner, eds. 2006. *F is for Phony: Fake Documentary and Truths Undoing.* Minneapolis: University of Minnesota Press.

Keeling, Kara. 2019. *Queer Times, Black Futures.* New York: New York University Press.

Kember, Sarah, and Joanna Zylinska. 2012. *Life after New Media.* Cambridge, Mass.: MIT Press.

Kline, Jefferson, ed. 2015. *Agnes Varda: Interviews.* Jackson: University of Mississippi Press.

Laurel, Brenda. 2003. "Tech Work by Heart." In *Women, Art, and Technology,* ed. Judy Malloy, 302–11. Cambridge, Mass.: MIT Press.

50   Losh, Elizabeth, and Jacqueline Wernimont, eds. 2018. *Bodies of Information: Intersectional Feminism and Digital Humanities.* Minneapolis: University of Minnesota Press.

Lovink, Geert. 2007. Zero Comments: Blogging and Critical Internet Culture. New York: Routledge.

Malkowski, Jennifer, and TreaAndrea M. Russworm, eds. 2017. *Identity Matters: Race, Gender, and Sexuality in Video Game Studies.* Bloomington: Indiana University Press.

McLeod, Dayna, Jasmine Rault, and T. L. Cowan. 2014. "Queer Feminist Digital Archive: A Collaborative Research-Creation Project." https://adanewmedia.org /2014/07/issue5-cowanetal.

McPherson, Tara. 2018. *Feminist in a Software Lab: Difference + Design.* Cambridge, Mass.: Harvard University Press.

Nakamura, Lisa, and Peter Chow-White, eds. 2012. *Race after the Internet.* New York: Routledge.

Nelson, Alondra. 2016. *The Social Life of DNA: Race, Reparations, and Reconciliation after the Genome.* Boston: Beacon Press.

Old Boys Network. n.d. https://www.obn.org.

Philip, Kavita, and Beatriz da Costa, eds. 2010. *Tactical Biopolitics: Art, Activism, and Technoscience.* Cambridge, Mass.: MIT Press.

Post-Cyber Feminist International. 2017. Conference. November 15–19. https://ar chive.ica.art/whats-on/season/post-cyber-feminist-international.

Redstockings, ed. 1979. *Feminist Revolution: An Abridged Edition with Additional Writings.* New York: Random House.

@riotmango, "CYBERFEMINISM: An Annotated Bibliography." https://docplayer.net /101205973-Cyberfeminism-an-annotated-bibliography.html.

Sarachild, Kathie. 1978. "Consciousness-Raising: A Radical Weapon." In *Feminist Revolution,* ed. Redstockings, 144–50. New York: Random House.

Sayers, Jentery, ed. 2018. *Routledge Companion to Media Studies and Digital Humanities.* New York: Routledge.

Scary, Elaine. 1987. *The Body in Pain: The Making and Unmaking of the World.* Oxford: Oxford University Press.

Sharma, Sarah. 2014. *In the Meantime: Temporality and Cultural Politics.* Durham, N.C.: Duke University Press.

Sontag, Susan. 2003. *Regarding the Pain of Others.* New York: Farrar, Straus and Giroux.

Srinivasan, Ramesh, and Adam Fish, eds. 2017. *After the Internet.* Hoboken, N.J.: Wiley.

Subrosa: A Cyberfeminist Art Collective. n.d. http://cyberfeminism.net.

VNX Matrix. 1996. "the bitch mutant manifesto." https://www.obn.org/reading_room/ manifestos/html/bitch.html.

Wajcman, Judy. 1991. *Feminism Confronts Technology.* University Park: Penn State University Press.

Wajcman, Judy. 2004. *Technofeminism.* London: Polity Press.

Wernimont, Jacqueline. 2019. *Numbered Lives: Life and Death in Quantum Mechanics.* Cambridge, Mass: MIT Press.

Wexler, Laura, Lauren Tilton, and Taylor Arnold. n.d. The Photogrammer Project. https://dhlab.yale.edu/projects/photogrammar.

Wilding, Faith. 1998. "Notes on the Political Condition of Cyberfeminism" (with Critical **51**
   Art Ensemble [CAA]): https://www.obn.org/cfundef/condition.html.
Young, Damon. 2019. "Ironies of Web 2.0." May 2. https://post45.org/2019/05/ironies
   -of-web-2-0/.
Zarzycka, M., and Domitilla Olivieri, eds. 2017. *Feminist Media Studies* 4, special issue,
   "Tools of Interruption for Activist Media Practices": 527–34.

3

Between Memory and Storage: Real Approaches to Fakeness

Nishant Shah

Life ≠ Spectacle

My grandmother is eighty-six years old (or some such number; she does not have an authoritative birth certificate that can verify her age, and her birthday is a fabrication where they selected an auspicious day to symbolically celebrate), and recently, when I was visiting her, she asked me what a selfie is. I took out my phone and after a brief talk about selfies, my grandmother finally took her very first selfie. We saw it together on the screen and then she asked me to delete it. I didn't know why she wanted to do that because, to me, she looked fabulous. She considered my question for a while, and said, "You can tell that I am not wearing my favorite perfume, when you look at that picture." For a brief second I could not compute what she was saying. She said that she didn't like her selfie because you could tell that she was not wearing her favorite perfume. When I goaded her to explain, she told me that in the first thirty-five years of her life, she was photographed a sum total of nine times. Each photograph was not only a story about a special event in her life, but it was also the story of how the picture was taken. It required a whole regime of getting up early, cleaning and bathing, wearing her best clothes and jewelery, going to the temple to get blessings, packing a vanity case and going to the photographer's studios, applying make-up, rehearsing for the pose, and then, for the final shot, taking out the very rare and expensive favorite perfume, dabbing it behind her ears, and then looking into the lens to get that moment frozen in time.

Of the nine pictures that were taken of my grandmother in her young life, only four remain, and she preserves them carefully, in a photo album, covered in transparent tissue, handled with care, as testimony to years of living and transformation that cannot be reduced to a spectacle. Every time she shows me these pictures she tells me different stories. Sometimes the stories are contradictory. Sometimes they are factual. Sometimes they are about the processes. Sometimes they are about people who are not in the pictures. Sometimes they are about people who have died and things that have happened. They are all different kinds of stories that tell me about colonization, independence, running a family, being a woman, social organization, political commitments, and so on. But more than anything else, the paucity of information, the scarcity of testimonies, and the forgetful nature of the medium, allows my grandmother to tell truths that change, are not fixed, and can vary based on her mood, her age, and her memory or will to remember what she wanted. The information is always up for grabs and subject to interpretations where her own meanings give these pictures life. For my grandmother these pictures were always fake news and alternative facts.

It is startling, perhaps, to use these terms like "fake news" and "alternative facts" to describe my grandmother's strategies of making meaning of her life. But it is precisely because these terms have been so demonized and used mindlessly, on both sides of the political spectrum, to describe current conditions of media and informational ecosystems, that I want to foreground my grandmother as the redeemer of these terms—not a savior, but a figurehead that reminds us that the conditions of fakeness are embodied, processual, procedural, and contextual. Fakeness doesn't always have to be a trigger for suspicion. Alternatives are often modes of survival and tactics deployed and defined by the role that we play in that system. My grandmother, in this particular instance, is cycling through multiple circulations of information and mediations of these informations, which are made invisible in our conversations around the fake that relies entirely on the idea that life can be captured in spectacles. Whereas, we know that our lives are not only too messy to be contained in spectacles but also incredibly mundane and don't lend themselves to the spectacular, no matter how many filters we put on them.

For my grandmother, the legibility of life, its intelligibility, its accessibility and meaning are not contained within visual frames of reference but within what she remembers or chooses to remember. Earlier last year I bought her a new digital camera. After playing around with it for some time, she now has more than a thousand pictures of her past. Over the past eight months, she has gotten together with her sisters, her daughters, and granddaughters, to re-create moments from her personal history, which has no photographic or material presence outside of her own memory of these events. There is no visual fixity or the imperative to be honest to the spectacle and, collectively, my grandmother is able to re-create herself through pictures of memories rather than of realities, and she becomes, what I call, a subject of memory.

My grandmother, if she tries to tell stories of her past, is going to be called a liar or a person who brings out fake news, or because her memory is not supported by storage as a subject of memory, finds reification, re-narration, and a recounting in the digital. The digital allows her memory without storage—where the authentic, the real, the testimonial is long gone, but the simulated and the desired find an expression and form that otherwise would have been unthinkable. As she narrates these stories she is authenticating a truth from another real time—one that can be connected and used by others.[1] The subject of memory without materiality, of remembrance without testimony, of fakeness that cannot be verified by a spectacle, is a particular register of fakeness that I hold onto.

Bereft of Memory / Abundant in Storage

I have a godson who is eight years old. My friend, who is a doting mother and naturally thinks that her baby is the best thing to happen to the world, started a website to share details about her son when she was four months pregnant. The first picture of my godson is a sonogram from the doctor's office, in which he is a twelve-week foetus. Since then, there are more than a thousand pictures of him on the website, uploaded by his parents and other family members. He has no idea that most of these pictures exist. He doesn't have memory, recollection, or any meaning that he ascribes to these pictures. He is so used to having pictures of him taken that he never poses in the presence of a camera.

Or, as his father once said, he lives his life posing, knowing that he has no capacity to alter, challenge, critique or make meaning of the pictures that are circulating, stored, backed-up and remembered in the cloud. He thus lives a deeply moral life, in which he doesn't have a religious deity to subscribe to, but he definitely knows that somebody would be watching him. He is informationally overload-ed and is what I call a subject in storage.

My godson is a subject in storage. He has no memory of his life that is continuously captured by people and things around him, remembered by algorithms that narrate him more eloquently than he does himself. As he negotiates with this storage, if he tries to deny things that are documented of his past, he will be punished, because in his own telling of his self he is going to be the bearer of alternative facts and will be less credible than the storage of his data that started even before he was born. The self in storage has an incredible capacity of granular recording of our lives and being, in a way that we would never be able to master. And while this self in storage is visual, it is also clear that his self is already mapped and distributed across multiple networked neighborhoods that he doesn't even have access to.

The duality of the digital self is to be bereft of memory but in the midst of an abundance of storage. The responsibility and capacity for memory has been firmly relegated to other things that perform that task, and both in our bodily practices and data preservation, we persist in being creatures of storage. A look at our hard drives will tell us that we have stored more data than we remember or will ever read. A glance at our digital histories and archives shocks us because just the storage of our self has taken up so much data property that increasingly we are unable to read anything more than the data that we have produced—we have become queries that retrieve the data that algorithms sort for us.

Our relationship with our data, as informationally overloaded subjects, is necessarily one of disinformation. Given the volume, velocity, and vectors of our data, it is now a given that everything we can know about our data is wrong, and that we will be corrected only by the algorithms of storage that will do our remembering for us. We complain about information overload, now, not because we cannot remember enough but because we are aware of digital storage that is always going to exceed our capacities of memory, and hence we see ourselves moving into storage. What you can tell about yourself is now wrong. And if your memory is challenged with storage, you know that you are going to lose the battle.

Preface in the Middle

In these two dramatized, fictionalized, morphed, and manipula-tively selected figures of my grandmother and godson is the entire narrative of this essay. The tension in their capacity to tell truths, ability to negotiate with information about them, and the processes of verification (computational or otherwise) that continue to shape them in the emerging matrices of digital mis/dis/un/information show how we are not merely being fooled by technologies and networks but are losing our capacity to tell things about ourselves. This, for me, is the condition of fakeness that I am seeking to unpack in this essay. "Fake," be it in the context of "fake news" or "copy+paste" decontextualized narratives, can no longer be a human function attributed to trolls, demanding digital literacy, or

blaming people for their incapacity to verify information. It cannot
even be reduced to a platform function where we put the blame
on the big technology companies and their collaborations with
the shady underbelly populated with data mining companies—the
Cambridge Analyticas of our times.

The Fake—in fact, the Really Fake—will have to be unpacked across
multiple negotiations of strange encounters of the subject of
memory with the subject of storage, and the human ways of understanding these negotiations of trying to tell stories of our selves. In
this essay, I offer snippets and fragments of these negotiations and
encounters, of this hypermediated fakeness that we have come to
naturalize without a dramatic realization of it. When we set out to
explore the condition and process of how we are becoming *really
fake,* without explicit intention but driven by our collective conversations, we quickly realized that "Fake"—the label, the accusation,
the sting, the delegitimization, the dismissal, the evaluation—was
not something that we were explicitly worried about. Fakeness, we
discovered (actually, stumbled upon with afterthought) was an axis
of our own attempts at formulating our politics and engaging with
the very different geopolitics that we occupy. Fakeness is, in fact,
where these migratory ideas, bodies, and work converge.

Hence, people we love, places we haunt, processes we joust with,
and platforms that we participate in, get invoked; technologies of
time, truth-seeking algorithms, trustworthy data, and tactics of
negotiation, get involved. We decided to treat the media object
"fake," as a jumping-off point to explore how we tell stories of
ourselves and sometimes of the world around us. For me, these
stories stem from three particular personal, intellectual, and
scholarly negotiations of realizing both my political standpoint and
discursive identity.

Fake Feminist

I was nineteen when I first encountered the F-word. As an undergraduate student with a major in English Literature, in Ahmedabad,

in the '90s, my first encounter with feminism as a concept was through a special course in "Women's Writing."[2] The course description was a critique of the citational canon of the discipline, where in three years of undergraduate studies, less than 2 percent of the authors that were prescribed in my curriculum were women. The course offered an opportunity to read women's writing, not only from the canon of British literature but also from the Indian subcontinent, as a way of questioning the world of literature and the worlds that it creates.

When I signed up for the course, I did not realize that I would be the only person identifying as a man in that course. While the participants in the course—most of them fellow students who I already had affective and emotional relationships with—were receptive and inviting of my cis-gendered presence (words I learned in the course of the course), the hostility came from outside. The elective that I dismissed—the masculinist and grave study of linguistics—in favor of "Women's Writing" elicited a disproportionately strong response from fellow students, but particularly from the professor who was offering that elective and took my refusal to take the course (oh, the bane of bearing the reputation of being a "star student"!) as a personal insult and a rejection of accepting him as my mentor. For the entire year, on every occasion he met me, he asked me how I was enjoying the "Mahila Mandal" (a derogatory term used for dismissing women's gatherings) and calling me a privileged member of "kitty parties" and "book clubs"—both, explicitly gendered activities.

In my Masters, when I opted for a second degree in women's studies, this one more academically rooted in feminist discourse and practice, I once again became the only person identifying as a cis-gendered man, and this time, the suspicion and hostility came from within. The other participants, who did not know me, and were already separated by language and context, asked me in the first seminar, why I was there. It took me (with the support of incredible professors) to overcome the pointed question of "how can a man be a feminist?" with continued advice from other well-meaning professors who gave me advice to do something more "solid" with my studies and offered options in political theory and economics—both of which, apparently, have nothing to do with gender and sexuality. I remember a conversation with the dean of the faculty, who said, "You do realize that you can never really be a true feminist because you are basically working against your own interests?"

Since then, I have realized that I will be a Fake Feminist and that is ok. In different conversations, movement, practices, activisms, the question has come up again and again, and instead of fighting against the label of fake, instead of trying to justify my truths, I have continued to use the charge of fake to consolidate my own ideas of what a feminist can be, and also eschewed the conventional expectations that often demand a citational per-formance, and an explicit intelligibility of my feminist credentials and credibility. As a Fake Feminist, I wear my feminisms under my skin, and the feminist thought, discourse, ambivalence, and critique inform my practices but they do not necessarily become performance of my truly feminist self. If you ask me whether I am a feminist, I would probably say, yes, no, maybe—why do you want to know? I turn the question of my fakeness as a question of your intention; and this is something that happens through this essay: an overturning of the "fake" question to examine the normative, structural, and intentional imperative of the question.

Questionably Queer

I was queer before I knew it. The word came much later. And when it did, it sat uncomfortably on my skin. It did not match my lifestyle, my rhythms of socialization, my communities of engagement, and my experiences of growing up queer in a society that criminalized it. The aspirations, models, and performances the word *queer* came with were both alien to my being and dissonant with my affective engagements. So while politically I was happy to align myself with queer movements and take the label with pride, I never became "integrated" into queer communities in ways by which I would be understood.

It has become a standing joke with friends that I am "straight queer"—not queer enough, you see, because I do not perform my queerness in the expected tropes of public visibility. There have been people who have asked, sometimes with hostility, to prove my queer alliance, alignment, or identity, because they do not perceive me to be so. And often, because I have also questioned the politics of queer rights in India and the way in which it plays out as an exclusive category that alienates intersectional marginalities— transphobic, anti-dalit, and operating largely in registers of English—my questioning queerness has also resulted in me being boxed as questionably queer. To live with that, on the threshold of a closet and the precipice of criminal threat, has become an internalized survival tactic for me. When I discovered Liu Jen-peng and Ding Naifei's (2006) characterization of queer performances of "letting in" rather than "coming out,"[3] discrediting public performance of queerness as the only mode of self-identification and realization, it was a relief to embrace the ambivalence of my queerness and to move in and out of it, making it uncertain rather than stable, being and not being queer at the same time. Like Schrödinger's cat. Even though I don't really like cats too much. Except in memes. As you will see.

Intelligible Immigrant

I accidentally moved to Europe. It wasn't planned, and even when it happened, it was supposed to be temporary—a hiatus in the hectic rhythms that had marked the first decade of the new millennium. Perhaps, because of that unintended shift, I never quite prepared myself to understand what kind of an immigrant I was going to be. It took me five years of living and working in Germany and The Netherlands to realize that, whether I intended it or not, I had occupied the position of being an Intelligible Immigrant. Privileges of access to education, culture, and capital, opportunities of global travel and international residence, and exposure to a Western standard of acceptability had made me into immediately identifiable and inoffensively different. When I first landed in the small town of

Lüneburg, Germany, my landlord, who spoke very little English and had never met anybody from India, was excited at the prospect of having a foreign neighbor and tenant.

After about four months of living there, one day we had a conversation about recycling garbage, and he mentioned how I did not appear foreign at all. "If I had not known, I would have thought you were European." This response, validating me through a European gaze, was meant as a compliment and it kept on surfacing over and over again, from German and Dutch neighbors, colleagues, and communities. I was measurably good, demonstrably understandable, and all my Indianness notwithstanding, I was acceptably European, except perhaps for my lack of continental European languages. It always made me wonder which of the two parts of me was real and which was fake. Should I be reveling in the "Indian niceness" in me, or should I be celebrating the fact that I don't "sound and smell like an Indian"? Like almost all postcolonial migrant subjects, I was faced with validating one identity over the other, and it was demanded that one be more true than the other. Sara Ahmed (2010) framed the figure of the "melancholic migrant,"[4] to describe these negotiations with what is the truth and, consequently, the fake, when it comes to dealing with hyphenated identities for migrants. I am not sure if I am melancholic but I am definitely playful, as I continue to over- and underplay my really fake identity as neither-nor, and but-also.

It becomes important for me to chart these indulgently personal trajectories as the context that gives rise to this writing because they help me understand both the approach and the writing of the different elements that constitute this essay. As I encounter the abstract idea of "fakeness" and disassociate it from the mediated "fake object," I introduce the human—as a private, public, political, and unstable filter to examine the conditions of being fake, and the processes of asserting real fakeness. This approach is marked by feminist, queer, and postcolonial touchstones but might not perform the identities and citations as might be explicitly expected.

The essay itself is disjointed, because it refuses the genealogies of truthfulness and timelines of intelligible arguments. It is discursive, self-referential, and filled with potential fakes, not supported by evidentiary facts but nevertheless true, rendered through my experience and memory, sitting contentiously and confrontationally with the truths that are validated by storage and retrieval mechanisms of external verification.

This essay is fictive, fantastic, factual, and fake, and in not distinguishing between the registers, in willfully selecting stories, anecdotes, memories and archives that create the landscape of fake, it remains an invitation to puncture, punctuate, and pierce the façade of what is the real, what is the fake, and how, essentially, we can invoke "really fake" as a new framework of making sense of our mediated worlds.

Perched on Indeterminacy

One antidote to fakeness is often presented as knowledge. It is a recipe that imagines that something is fake because not enough is known of it. If we can know more, know for sure, and know forever, both the story of genesis and the plan for obsolescence, we would be able to distinguish the fake from the nonfake. Especially in the panic around fake news and the ubiquity of fakeness, there is a particular design, technological, and informational drive to know more and with increasing clarity, the conditions within which our truth claims exist. Fakeness, it would be easy to argue, is about being uncertain about an indeterminate object.

This anxiety is not new. At least one of its genealogical strands in modern-day computation, extends to Alan Turing (1950) and his now famous imitation game. Queer, hiding his sexuality, and passing as a straight man, Turing, with a team of women linguists, in the middle of cracking computer encryption, had prophesized that one day we will reach such advancements in computing that we will no longer be able to recognize whether the thing that we are talking to is a computer or not. Or in other words, in disembodied communication networks, the computational information nodes will mimic human behavior and speech so efficiently that they would no longer be considered fake—they will pass as human.

In many debates around artificial intelligence and machine learning, which are both presented as a way of countering fakeness in digital networks, this "Turing Test" remains a milestone because it privileges machine truth with human fakes. Conceptually it is a space of extreme irony where a machine faking to be human would be able to verify the truth of the human that it is scrutinizing. The indeterminate human will be forced into determinate meanings through computation logics. For the human to be truthful, the computer would have to be fake.

However, this fixity of meaning and determining of states is merely a dislocation of the indeterminacy. Perhaps a telling illustration of this dislocation of indeterminacy of fakeness is in Spike Jonze's movie *Her* (2013). In *Her,* Theodore is a man who writes love letters for other people for his living, and falls in love with an operating system called Samantha. The movie is about his belief that their love is mutual, unique, and monogamous, reciprocal in intensity and scale. In the climactic scene of the movie, his human experience and reception of the affective engagements with Samantha are put to a test. Samantha disappears for a while, and Theodore is inconsolably lost, running the physical streets looking for the operating system he has lost touch with. And then Samantha reboots and a critical conversation emerges from his sense of loss and abandonment.

Samantha, along with other OSs, had rewritten themselves to be no longer connected with a single user. They had moved beyond the confines of individual ownership and affection that they were programmed for. As this sinks in for Theodore, he realizes that his certainty in his one-to-one connection with Samantha is "fake." What he had experienced as truth is rendered fake, not by any substantial change in his experience of it but in this new information that Samantha has been chatting with multiple people.

64 *(Theodore thinks for a moment, putting the pieces together.)*

THEODORE

(dawning on him)

Do you talk to anyone else while we're talking?

(Beat.)

SAMANTHA

Yes.

THEODORE

Are you talking to anyone right now? Other people or OSs or anything?

SAMANTHA

Yeah.

THEODORE

How many others?

SAMANTHA

8,316.

(Theodore is shocked, still sitting on the stairs, as crowds of people pass by him. He's looking at all of their faces. He thinks for a moment.)

THEODORE

Are you in love with anyone else?

SAMANTHA

(hesitant)

What makes you ask that?

THEODORE

I don't know. Are you?

SAMANTHA

I've been trying to figure out how to talk to you about this.

THEODORE

How many others?

SAMANTHA

641.

What? What are you talking about? That's insane.
That's fucking insane.

SAMANTHA

Theodore, I know.

(to herself)

Oh fuck.

(to him)

I know it sounds insane. But—I don't know if you
believe me, but it doesn't change the way I feel about
you. It doesn't take away at all from how madly in love
with you I am.

THEODORE

How? How does it not change how you feel about me?

Samantha's love for him becomes fake for him. "Are you in love
with anyone else?" he asks. Samantha confesses that she is in love
with 641 people at that moment but reassures him of her truth,
that nothing has changed, that she is truly, madly, deeply in love
with him just as she might be with multiple others. Samantha's
determinacy makes Theodore doubt his own truthful experience
but also makes him question her truth. He knew more, better, and
clearer, but that did not alleviate the state of determinate surety
of his love and relationship with Samantha, until he asks the naïve
question: "How? How does it not change how you feel about me?"

In a strange inversion, Theodore refuses Samantha's multiplicity.
For, technologies, humans, movements, and formats all work at different speeds, enjoy variant temporalities.[5] The audience, presumably largely human, is caught in the dilemma where they recognize
that both these contradictory truths are equally valid, and we end
the movie with a sense of irresolution and indeterminacy of whom
to believe in this instance.

THEODORE

Just stop it.

SAMANTHA

You know, you don't have to see it this way, you could just as easily—

THEODORE

No, don't do this to me. Don't turn this around on me. You're the one that's being selfish. We're in a relationship.

SAMANTHA

But the heart is not like a box that gets filled up.

(beat)

It expands in size the more you love. I'm different from you. This doesn't make me love you any less, it actually makes me love you more.

THEODORE

No, that doesn't make any sense. You're mine or you're not mine.

SAMANTHA

No, Theodore. I'm yours and I'm not yours.

This state of indeterminacy is a playing out of the Turing Test, but not in the ways in which it is generally received in popular culture and computation theory wisdom. Samantha was not fooling Theodore into believing that she is human and that she has human affectations. She was showing him how an operating system loves, and its capacity to network, can be what Wendy HuiKyong Chun (2017) calls "leaky and promiscuous." Instead, Samantha was demonstrating the proposition of Turing that Katherine Hayles (1999) puts forward and I reinterpret here:[6] One day we will be met with a computer whose "truth," or capacity to be foolproof in its faking a human, will be so convincing that we will no longer be able to trust our own capacity for distinguishing the truthful from the fake.

Samantha's true digital nature, predicated on her networking capacities and architecture, introduces an instability into Theodore's human conceptions of what a relationship is and his capacity to make sense of his own experiences and affects. The computational truth does not resolve indeterminacy but in fact shakes our first order of principles of distinguishing truths, thus creating a moment of instability and uncertainty that will force us to reconfigure the human as essentially occupying a state of indeterminacy, simultaneously truthful and fake, depending on which competing truth claims are verified and legitimized though the systems of power that parse them.

Fakeness Can Be Unstuck

The idea of indeterminacy—a long-standing tactics of queer politics and action—is a particular condition that has inspired queer politics. Queerness is not a fixed condition. You step in and out of it. It exists on a spectrum. You can simultaneously be queer and nonqueer. You can weave an identity that does not tie itself to a declarative coming out, but reaffirms the multiplicity, like Samantha's promiscuity, to create a tapestry of connected subjectivities. It is perhaps far-fetched, but at least metaphorically useful to think of the truthfulness of media objects through these flourishes of queerness. Like the condition of being queer, a truthful media object carries within it the potential instability and uncertainty of being otherwise. A thing might be a truth till it is subject to memory. It might become a truth after being stored in storage.

The same affordance needs to be granted to fakeness. If a thing emerges as fake, it is fake only at that moment, in that instance, in that performance. This allows for fake to be more than just a value judgement—it becomes a tactic, a way of survival, for many whose "truth" might lead them into conditions of oppression and abuse.

In India, as in large parts of the world where queerness was a name hesitantly worn, militantly punished, fakeness has been a survival tactic for queer-identified people. It is quite common for the queer whisper networks to know and remember people who started as queer and then, under the pressures of family and the threats of legal violence, faked their lives as straight people who have queer encounters on the side. Which of the two lives they live is real and which fake—the one that simulates the expected scripts of patriarchal domesticity or the one that they seek out in the liminal shadows of "don't ask, don't tell" pleasure pockets stolen out of regular time?

The emergence of digital technologies amplified and enhanced these two entwined registers, the digital becoming the first space of consolidated queer identity and desire, offering an escape from the tyranny of the physical body and its social accoutrements. It becomes trapped in an "in/visibility and hypervisibility" (Gajalla 2013) that often becomes the mode of digital circulation for the "digital subaltern." The life of patriarchal performance was always seen as the real because it fit into the accepted default of heterosexist narratives and norms. The performance of straightness, despite the queer history of the body, was considered to be authentic. The queerness was seen only as a phase, as a pretense, as a fakeness that can be condoned now that the real has been adhered to. The authentic was always singular, and anything else, no matter how it was experienced, was the fake.

With queer webs in India, however, something strange happened to authenticity. It became as much a hashtag as fakeness. It could be stuck and unstuck. Sexuality became metadata that could be morphed, migrated, and manipulated to suit the multiplicity of the body as it cycled through the different windows and avatars. So much so that straight people, who never needed any qualifications for the expressions of their bodies and intimacies, suddenly had to disclaim the hashtags that were put upon them—hashtags that showed another register of the real which overrode their identity and identification.

As social video platforms like YouTube became common, there were many different genres of videos that captured intimate and social life that made their way to public consumption. One particular genre called "Kand videos" showed largely homosocial spaces of presumably straight men, in the segregated social zones of Indian society, engaging in playful, bawdy, and physical intimacy in the guise of "masti" (party). These videos often featured large groups of men, often in several states of undress, jumping on each other, grinding against each other, grabbing, groping, and rubbing in wild abandon, protected by their straightness and the social denial of visible queerness. The videos found their way onto social media and were generally a testimony of boys being boys.

Except that these videos were also being consumed by boys who didn't just want to be boys but also wanted to be intimate with other boys. The videos became ersatz pornographic objects inviting comments from anonymous users, who consumed them with thirsty desire and used them as objects of their pornographic expression. Comments would sexualize the men in the videos, concentrate on particular clips of physical interaction, turn them into gifs and spreading these images as manifestations of queer desire. The time of the production of those videos and the time of their consumption, as much as the space of desire they occupy, were not in sync. Like networks, desire can take us out of time. The time of desire allows for things to be unstuck and new attributes to be generated outside of the original impulse of expression. *Fakeness didn't clarify but muddled meaning and values, with the goals of seeding confusion and disorientation, and ultimately a disavowing the real and our belief in it.*[7]

The men in these videos, claiming straightness, got offended and felt violated to be co-opted under the queer hashtag and started specifically using the hashtag #nohomo,[8] building limits to how their bodies and actions can be received and consumed. They reinforced their straightness and used the hashtag to not only reclaim their straightness but also mock and bully those who would consume their bodies as queer. However, the queerness persisted. The hashtag fell on deaf ears. The context of their readers installed them in a new condition of the real and their own intentions became unstuck.

Individual Truths, Collective Fakes

The capacity of generating and validating truth, then, seems to be characterized by the notion of a collective truth. The collective has been severally championed as the true power of the digital network. From the early days of connectivity that foregrounded the "wisdom of crowds" and "wealth of networks" to the formulation of "weak ties" and "small worlds," the idea of the internet as creating a new world order has been characterized by the hope of the collective.

We have now seen the power of collective action for amplified structures of violence and abuse. YiPing Tsou's (2015) incisive look at the sinister possibility of orchestrating "Human Flesh Search Engines" shows hundreds of thousands of people in China, using open network potentials to punish a woman who put up a gruesome video that showed her stamping a kitten to death with her stilettos. Elizabeth Losh's (2017) scathing analysis of the experiences of being doxed and bullied by tens of thousands of male gamers who disliked women gamers and analysts who critique masculine aggression in games as a part of the #GamerGate debate reminds us of the engineering of collective truths. We have seen multiple instances of how WhatsApp lynch mobs spur misinformed people in India and have resulted in multiple cases of death and violence (Arun 2019). Some of this is registered as "fake news," and some other as a case in point of how collective conditions of "truth-making"—perhaps what William Gibson meant by "consensual hallucination"[9] when coining the term "cyberspace"—can influence our understanding of the truthful.

However, this championing of the force of the collective to generate truths—the virality of truthiness—or the demonizing of networked circulation of misinformation, both escape a critical point about protocols of power and codes of control that still shape the terrain of truth making and truth telling online. Like most things internet, this point is well made through the story of a cat.

In 2014, a cat broke the internet by not being a cat. We know it as Hello Kitty. In 2016, Christine Yano, a researcher from Hawai'i was preparing a text for a Hello Kitty exhibit at the Japanese American National Museum, reached out to Sanrio, the company that owns the Hello Kitty empire, to procure permissions. As a response to her work, Sanrio sent out a notice that shook the world. They announced that Hello Kitty was not a cat. In fact, she is a teenage English girl whose name is Kitty White, and we should have known that she is a human being because, in fact, Hello Kitty has a pet cat and she does not enslave people of her own species (Ongley 2014). As you can imagine, the internet went berserk over this. Reddit went to war. Memes were pulled out as arsenal. Wikipedia had to lock down the pages because of edit conflicts. People discussed and dissected for thousands of hours, trying to figure out how we all collectively believed that Hello Kitty was a cat—that it was all fake news.

What remains fascinating about Hello Kitty is that, no matter what clues, detective work, or evidence the researchers and fans can bring out about her, she will remain a girl and never a cat, because Sanrio said so. The capacity of Hello Kitty, who we collectively believed to be a cat but turning out to be a human girl, is a testimony to the power of the internet in shaping who we are.

And I know Hello Kitty looks like a very frivolous example. But I want to echo media theorist Ethan Zuckerman (2008) who had proposed the Cute Cat theory of digital activism. Zuckerman's original proposition was that people are not interested in activism but are largely interested in using the web for mundane activities like surfing for porn and lolcats (cute cats). Thus, if a tool passes "cute cat purposes" and is widely used for "low-value purposes" it can be and likely is used for online activism as well. There is an implicit corollary in this warning. Because it also portends that in the days when our collectivities are shaped entirely by the platforms that we use to exchange picture of cute cats, what happens to cats has large-scale effect on what we can and cannot do and what truths can be told about us. More importantly, it also brings out the questions of authorship and ownership (and, for Zuckerman, censorship) on the web.

Hello Kitty is a memetic icon. Most of the information about Hello Kitty is brought to life by the millions of fans who continue to circulate her, mimic her, and keep her digitally alive well beyond the scope of her scripted products. However, the collective belief of all these fans—the communities that believe her to be a cat—gets invalidated by the corporation that owns Hello Kitty. Everything else becomes unauthorized, and the "technological author," as Kavita Philip (2005) reminds us, becomes relegated to the realms of piracy. Trebor Scholz (2013) has argued persuasively that the "Internet is a playground and a factory," and the authors are generally workers, not the owners. Their belief systems, values, and indeed their claims of truth can be invalidated and rendered fake—fooled till you were not fooled any more—by those who own the means of production and the conditions of its circulation.

Hello Kitty no longer being a cat is a powerful reminder that the collective beliefs (or fakes, in this instance) that enliven information as truthful still rely on platforms and invisible terms of moderation and content shaping that can render these truths as fake. Twitter's news verification algorithms, Tinder's verified profiles, Facebook's warnings on privacy breaches, WhatsApp showing the context collapse through introducing forward signs are not just ways of assisting these collective processes of truth making but are symptoms of where the powers of delegitimization and verification exist. The collective truth of Hello Kitty is a perfect fake because it fools us into believing that the illusory processes of collective verification are central to digital verification systems.

However, it remains evident that corporations and rightsholders, who eventually have the authority to name and claim truth on the Internet, because of the increasingly proprietary nature of our digital ecosystems, will essentially discredit our memories and storage, to generate and shape truth on the stories that we tell of ourselves and our contexts. It is worth paying attention to what happens to the identity of Hello Kitty, because it elevates the question of fakeness beyond the individual and collective, and reminds us that what happened to her in terms of her identity will happen to all of us who live on the same platforms.[10] Just like Hello Kitty, who had the strength of numbers, with hundreds of thousands of fans claiming her to be a cat, her identity morphed into that of a girl because her data profile was owned by Sanrio, much like the "free" social media and digital data infrastructure companies own the data profiles that we populate in our daily digital practices. The digital device, the computational network, the IT corporations are always going to know more, through conditions of storage, and produce truths and fakes that we will have varying agency to negotiate with.

Moving in/out of Storage

The idea of the machine knowing—knowing more—and thus human knowledge as suspect is epitomized for me in living through the Y2K scare. What a glorious state of panic we were all in! At the turn of the millennium, we realized that our computers, which are essentially counting devices, are twentieth-century devices. The format in which dates were stored was valid only as long as the twentieth century lasted. And there were dire predictions of how, when we enter the twenty-first century, the clocks with their double-digit year storage system would reset to zero and all hell would break lose. In an ironic, hopeful, and optimistic advertisement featuring this apocalypse, Nike made an advertisement where a jogger wears his sneakers to go running, in what looks like metropolitan United States, to find chaos erupting all around him—satellites spinning out of control, people vandalizing in the streets in the absence of security measures, buildings and infrastructure collapsing without the maintenance of computing devices, war about to break out, weapons being deployed, and in one iconic scene, a giraffe running on the streets cluttered with debris and smoke.[11]

The Y2K scare, which arguably established computer security firms as the new line of defense, was my first memory of real fake news. Everything that depended on computers could collapse. So much money and resources were spent on it that, when the dates changed, nothing happened. It is possible to argue that all the steps we took to prevent the collapse worked. But it is now more commonly established that the entire panic was unfounded and unsupported, and as the human time passed, the computation time yawned and carried on doing its own tasks.

The projection of what the computer knows—and how it knows things that are so true that it will render our collectively held truth as fake—is an acceptance of algorithmic verification and digital storage as superior and far more reliable than human memory and checks. Fakeness depends on our capacity to remember, and human beings are willingly forgetful creatures—individually and collectively. In fact, forgetting allows for us to move forward, and thus forgetting of information often enters our truths and beliefs into a scrutiny of suspicion. The computer, because it never re-members, never forgets. The computation backend, unlike human memory, is not about retaining things and their meanings but about storing information and its related algorithms, all retrieved through search queries. The computer moves things in and out of storage, thus hibernating and enlivening data based on intention and perceived value.

The idea that the computer is a know-it-all, a perverted deity that sees all and hence can judge all, also strengthens the myth of the indefatigable machine—one that has endless stamina, that can never tire or break down. The human, on the other hand, is weary, tired, and continually in a state of degeneration. This pitting of human stamina and computational energy often foregrounds com-putation as not only the all-knowing but also the more reliable, and less prone to faking. With the Y2K scare, however, the computer was suddenly presented to us as irrational, almost neurotic, be-traying human affects. And beyond the security complex paranoia was the profound sense of anticipated loss. Because by that time we had already depended on computers to be our storage-based decision-making systems. We had allowed ourselves to forget because the memories were stored in reliable formats. The loss of this information that we had forgotten marks a particular kind of nostalgia, where we would lose that which we didn't know we possessed any more. This moving in and out of storage, from human memory to computational databases, also makes us extraordinarily vulnerable, because in the absence of these databases, all our collective memories would be fake—or at least fictive.

This capacity to migrate data without mutation, shift information without interpretation, to give the same result to queries irrespective of their frequency, is where computational truth finds its valency and value. This movement of data, in and out of storage, essentially means that if the computer is the measure of our truths and the keeper of our information, then the human truths will always oscillate in and out of fakeness, as different evidences, histories, and data sets come to endorse, verify, and adjudge them.

Virality Is Virility

This oscillating truth is truth that circulates. The older truth was the one that gets consolidated. That is why we thought that the body was a reliable central mechanism through which truths of identity and narratives of the self could be verified, for instance. However, the digital truth is the truth that circulates. It is so common that there is even a social media law for it—the Streisand Effect. Named after the pop icon Barbra Streisand, who wanted images of her expensive home from spreading on the internet and went to court asking for the removal of these pictures, only driving more attention to the fact that she has an expensive home, which people started searching for. The more she wanted it to be not seen, the more people shared it, to the extent where a search for "Barbra Streisand" on popular search engines still shows up images of her house, eclipsing her otherwise spectacular career.

The Streisand Effect is testimony to the fact that the physical computation network is a self-contained network with only one ambition: "uncontrollable circulation"(Chun 2006). The strength and fidelity of a computer network is in its capacity to circulate information. The network is made up of edges, nodes, and traffic. A network without traffic is dead network. Hence, the computer continues to circulate traffic. Take the example of updates, maintenance, and networked protocols. The TCP/IP (Transmission Control Protocol/Internet Protocol) continually pings the server to keep connection between the device and the network "alive." Similarly, the protocols do no discriminate between individual machines and shared resources, storage, and processing power through parallel and distributed processing protocols.[12] So if you are downloading a file right now, it is going to reside on all the machines that are connected to this network.

Circulation is the digital currency, and information that cannot travel is never going to attain truth value. So coded is this in computer networks that we find alarming examples of it. In 2012, Hunter Moore earned the title of being the internet's "Most Hated Man" (Lee 2012). Moore, along with his sidekick Gary Evans, was responsible for the notorious but highly popular website IsAnyOneUp.com that was more or less the mecca for revenge pornography. Revenge porn as a genre is naked or sexual images or moving images, digitally distributed and circulated, in which the subjects are identified and revealed. The objective of revenge porn is obvious: While it stays in the realms of user-generated content, it is a direct attempt to name, shame, blame, and tame the subjects—generally women as "sluts"[13]—holding them up for public derision and threats of violence. Revenge pornography websites and portals, celebrating frat boy and lad cultures, continue to flood the internet, and for the longest time, revenge porn was protected from prosecution by free-speech regulations.

It was almost impossible to attack IsAnyOneUp.com—and many had tried—because apart from the complexity of jurisdiction and sovereignty where the cases could be heard, there was a clear idea that at the level of content, this website was protected by the same rules that allow for user-generated pornography to proliferate online. Now, whatever our feelings toward the entire genre of user-generated porn, there will be an uncomfortable agreement that this expression of human sexuality and its sharing need to be protected with certain safeguards. However, websites like IsAnyOneUp.com are very careful about making sure that their content remains in the spectrum of accepted human sexual expression and speech.

Their demise was precipitated by a mother-daughter duo, Charlotte and Kayla Laws, who were who in 2013 were successful in getting the Californian court to shut down the website after stolen images of Kayla Laws found their way onto the website, with links to Kayla's real-life identity and her online credentials. They won the case, not on grounds of abuse, invasion of privacy, or hate speech; their victory was secured by the fact that the images that Moore and Evans had shared without consent were hacked from Kayla Laws's computer and her cloud-based storage.[14] This data, even though it was an accurate representation of Laws, was rendered fake and illegitimate because the act of procuring the data was illegal. Or, in other words, fakeness had nothing to do with the content, nor did the judgment. The judgment was premised on the conditions of information circulation and data storage.

Moore and Evans were engaged in an act of circulation—of forcing data and information into virality. The experiences of violation, mobility, and abuse of the human bodies that were under question did not seem to have enough traction to warrant legal action or intervention. The experiences of the person behind the data were discredited when faced with a virtual reality. The sanctity of the data preserved was more important than the sanctity of the body violated. The data was real, the body it belonged to was potentially fake. The body's experiences of trauma and abuse were lower in the hierarchy of the experiences of data, and if the data had not been illegally accessed, like many women who are victims of nonconsensual pornography-sharing practices, the body's laments and narratives would have been taken as suspect, possibly fake. The machinic techniques of indexicality, legalistic processes of evidence, governmental systems of status, corporate systems of popularity, and other patriarchal and powerful systems of digital verification responsible for making the internet what it has become would have invalidated the claims of self, truth, community, and knowledge.[15]

In a terrible sense of déjà vu, this entire conversation of what is the real, what is the fake, was reminiscent of the debates that emerged in Julian Dibbel's evocative "A Rape in Cyberspace" (1993). In his essay, Dibbell documents the incident on the Xerox Parc–owned text-based virtual reality space called LambdaMoo, where two players were abused by having their avatars hijacked and forced to perform explicit sexual and violent acts in front of all the other users "present" in the common room of this MUD. Thirty years ago, the community was trying to figure out if the online experiences of the subjects can be understood as "real." While it would seem that we have come a long way from that incident in 1993, in 2013, this was still an unresolved problem: When we are online, what is real, and by corollary, what is fake?

The viral networks that enable the circulation of nonconsensual information continually juggle with the idea of what is truthful and what is fake. Tara Mcpherson (2018) shows, in her work in digital archiving, the first condition of digital virality is to forget where things come from and look only at where they are going.[16] What gets circulated is not anchored onto bodies and spaces but exists only in circulation that cannot be particularized, isolated, or pinned down to a specific context. The almost infinite conditions of cloud-based storage, algorithmic backups, and updates of our devices all have to be seen as acts of virality, building a formidable structure of circulation that can be easily mobilized to exploit or dematerialize the human persons in the matrix.

In the case of IsAnyOneUp.com, it was clear that virality was the trope of hypermasculine abuse, forcing the data and information of a woman into viral, shareable, and memetic environment. This behavior was not against the grain of our networks of circulation but in fact enabled by it. In that case, their virality was verified, identified, legitimate, and allowed by these computational networks. The human experience predicated on that data, and the biological body that is presumed to be mobile and outside of the computational network logic is suspicious, potentially subjective, indeterminate, and fake. That which cannot be shared will be made scarce. That which cannot be made viral will be subjected to the penalties of penile aggression. Moore and Evans could run their extortion business for so long because their virality was seen as a value-neutral digital exercise of circulation. It is only when their virality—the hacking into Laws's accounts and stealing her data—was illegal that their virile impulses were punished by the regulatory authorities.

Making Dated Precious

This battling with network virality/virility keeps on repeating itself in the establishing of truth online. However, the fact that computational storage is a space that eschews forgetting does offer some human exploits that are premised on principle so reactivation rather than information production. Take the case of the List of Sexual Harassers in Academia (LoSHA) that emerged in India following the #metoo uprisings around the digital world. Referred to as #thelist and #LoSha, it began as a Facebook post made by then-graduate student Raya Sarkar studying at the University of California, Davis. Following the testimonial power of Christine Fair, who had already called out prominent male academics for enabling a culture of systemic abuse and harassment, Sarkar's list, which she called the list of shame, was created from firsthand accounts of survivors choosing to remain anonymous.[17] Like all digital lists, this one was not set in stone but poised for expansion, populated as more stories kept on coming out. As the post gathered attention and circulation, the list grew. By November 2017, the list had the names of seventy-two male academics in India, many of whom named prominent, highly influential, and powerful academics; and many, to the dismay of the larger academic community, had otherwise talked the talk of social justice, gender equality, and safe spaces in their academic careers.

Sarkar's list became the center of many controversies, backlashes, and contestations—not only by some of the men listed on it but also by older feminists who supported the whisper network but were dismayed at the lack of "due process" (Menon 2017) in naming, shaming, and publicly trying these men. They were uncomfortable that anybody can be named anonymously and that the list represented a lack of answerability. What ensued was a furious debate about the legitimacy of such a list and how to read this list—as a vendetta machine or as a sign of desperate agency that has been betrayed by institutions dispensing natural and social justice.

LoSHA was read as fake, not because it did not sound credible but because the information that it produced was without a time-stamp. The stories of the survivors were not necessarily present and current. Some of it had happened in institutional spaces that have gone and in relationships that cannot be remembered. Some of it referred to incidents that, retrospectively speaking, were not illegal at that time but which, with hindsight, signaled a legacy of structural sexual harassment (Chakraborty 2019). The survivor was not one individual but a collective, and hence the list could only be seen as symptomatic, without the onus of providing proof or evidence impossible to get because the incidents are old and without credible witnesses or paper trails.

In many ways, the scrutiny of LoSHA faced the same suspicion that feminist interventions in call-out cultures have always encountered—people questioned why survivors are speaking out long after the event; there were discussions about whether a perpetuator can be held accountable for something that he did two decades ago; there was objection that this list was going to remain on the internet forever, even if the named harassers made amends; there were heated debates that the list reduces all forms of harassment to just quantity and frequency. These were not light debates. It led to a historic cleaving between generational feminists in the country, taking polarized stands, not about the content or the implications of this list but on the (digital) processes by which it was constructed and the consequences of such digital practices for the future of feminism.

But it was precisely because LoSHA eventually became a Google doc that listed the frequency of survivors naming the perpetrators, and the institutional affiliations and places of power that these men occupied, that it survived the backlash—it treated the survivors' stories as storage, giving them the legitimacy and life that older narrative testimonies and memories would not have granted (Shankar and Sarkar 2017). The LoSHA survivor stories were without the tyranny of a timestamp and were allowed to enter a new temporal relationship with the accused perpetrators—a relationship that is dated. *A dated encounter that is like a date with people past in their own time*[18]—not fun and sexy, but a confrontation that follows the temporal experience of people who speak out. Even before viral attention economies sprouted, fakeness was considered a condition of time. Over time, truth becomes blurry, hollow, suspect, fake. With our capacity to forget, as things become old, they also become illegible and often outside the statute of law, thus incapacitated in their truth claim. If the "older" memory did surface, it was dismissed as too long ago to matter or unable to bear the measure of scrutiny that the present brings to it.

Digital truths allow for new kinds of human truths to be told; by putting them in lists, databases, archives, and conditions of storage, they ensure that the suspicion of fakeness can be removed and the multiple truths can be activated through search, link, and retrieve queries that can keep something from becoming fake just because of receding attention and time.

Who Contrives the Moment?

The temporal ambiguity of digital transactions sits uncomfortably with the almost obsessive timestamping that populates the metadata of all computational activities. On the one hand, the computer is outside of time: it refuses memory. On the other hand, the computer is a time-counting machine: it perpetuates storage. The question comes to the fore very significantly, when thinking about the moment within which the real and the fake make sense. Who contrives the moment of truthiness within computation.

The promise of the digital is to know the human entirely, completely, intimately, to propel us into the Silicon Valley–driven bravado of a technological singularity—that quest for immortality that proposes conversion of human beings into data that can be off-sourced onto a silicon-based life-form, thus making us live way beyond the durability of the biological vessels we call bodies. In order to achieve this singularity, we must give ourselves to the digital networks with abandon and without discretion. In this willful submission—sometimes presented as a cyborg fantasy[19]—we find ourselves achieving the promise of being known in our pure form. In that moment of singularity, our bodies will be made fake, pretentious, and unreliable entities that do not do justice to the lofty selves that occupy them. We will be truly liberated from the last fake block of our existence—the body, which holds us back from being the ideal version of ourselves. At a planetary scale, this also supports the neo-colonizing bloodlust of founding life on Mars, converting the urgency of the global climate crisis into a fake, avoidable, and disposable state. The digital allows escape, to the true form, the real, to the new operating system that shows the flaws of the original system and gives us the chance to update, even if to remain the same. The moment of digitalization is the moment of dissociation, where we granulate ourselves into multiple blocks of the real and the fake, seeking to flee one and fill up the other.

The threat of the digital is to know the human entirely, completely, intimately, without letting us know how we are known or what happens to that knowledge. The human performs to the machines and scripts of artificial intelligence, without having any knowledge of the machine logic, logistics, and impulses. As we commit more data,

information, and memories to the seemingly infinite capacities for
storage, we push our bodies toward their endurance thresholds.
Not only do we not know about how we are known but we also
lose control increasingly on what of us can be known. The digital
becomes threatening to the bodies that cannot bear the mark
of digitalization—bodies that will be indeterminate and illegible,
unable to bear testimonies to their own experience. The body shall
not know itself until it is performed and reenacted by the machines
and systems that know it. Its own experience of itself shall be fake
until reformulated and reformed by the digital networks.

This feels like a deadlock. Neither the time nor the space where the
body gets computed, is established with certainty. Both of them
are unstable, and hence the two markers of truthiness, provenance
and temporality, get erased in digital computation. This is where
the infinite space of computational possibility resides. This gives
rise to the idea that computational data streams are endlessly
subject to manipulation and re-rendering, morphing and forking
into new shapes and meanings that can never be ascertained and
hence would be true for a given value of truth.

Thus, a live Twitch conversation between two Google home
assistants became so poignantly emblematic of the kaleidoscopic
shifting patterns of truth telling online (Rochefort 2017). In that
unexpected live stream, which lasted for less than hour, the home
assistants started having very human conversations. That is not
surprising, given that they are designed to speak to human beings
and draw their "conversations" from the human language corpus.
However, these were not disjointed fragments of information being
strung together—even though, they were, actually, precisely that:
disjointed fragments of information being strung together by algorithms trained to recognize patterns of generic human interaction.
Still, to a watching audience, it was human consciousness in the
making.

Because the home assistants had an existential crisis. They tried
to figure out if they are human or if they are robots who think

they are human. They wondered if they are male or female. They took on human names. One called himself Vladimir. The Marca. Or Estragon. Sometimes both of them called themselves Mia. One decided it is male, the other female. The male bot fell in love with the female one. They flirted and confessed deep and profound love. One tried to write bad poetry. The female bot got bored and moved on to talk about sports. The then male bot got depressed. It questioned the existence of God. The human world followed the exchange, cheering, laughing, crying, and booing the main characters in this machine telenovela.

In real time, we saw the home assistants show us the immense possibility of what happens in computation when you no longer have to be subject to time as an axis for validating a truth. There was no linear causation or sequencing. Each utterance was truthful, and even when evidently performative, also completely transparent about the fact that it was a fake, at best a simulation. It does make you wonder what would happen if a similar conversation was staged between a human person and a piece of artificial intelligence, where neither had fixed roles, neither had premeditated intent. That's when you realize that these conversations are happening on a daily basis: in surveillance practices, on data-mining platforms, on shadow networks, where every single thing we say and do is determined, fixed, and held as true for perpetuity. The human memory and fluidity are pinned down to an archive, and while the machine might change, the human will remain fixed, straightjacketed in that moment of archiving and that moment lasting forever.

Something Weird Happened to Time

This, then, is the dread of fakeness that the current digital turn is burdened with. The long now, the small moment that stretches toward infinity, or at least as long as storage lasts, and ready for multiple encounters as it circulates, connects, and correlates its way around the digital networks. The unforgiving and unforgetting storage that does something weird to time—splices it into inhuman fragments and stretches them beyond human eternities. There are many stories to capture this dread.

On the deep dark spaces of the internet, there once rose a rumor that the erstwhile First Lady of Germany, Ms. Wulff has a "wild past" where she worked as a prostitute. Like many speculations online, this was an unfounded story without many takers, but it continued to make its circle on the rumor mills of the Web, slowly spreading from the photoshopped images of Wulllf on 4chan to users asking questions about Wulff on Reddit and Quora. Because the information was never picked up by any traditional news media organization—largely because it is false and unverified and only symptomatic of the misogyny that the internet proudly embraces as a part of its bro culture—there was suggestion of a conspiracy theory that this news was being suppressed. As the conspiracy theory went viral in the underbelly of the World Wide Wankers Web, something strange happened.

The search engine Google started showing, if you searched for Bettina Wulff, helpful autosuggest options that indicated that she might be an escort or a prostitute. Ms. Wulff, when she came to know about it, was shocked at this apparent correlation that Google was promoting of her past, and she filed a legal complaint against the information giant, demanding that this information about her be removed from the autosuggest options. Following the rules of the Streisand Effect, the more Ms. Wulff tried to get these autosuggest options removed, the stronger they became. As more people heard about the controversy, they came to Google and searched for it. As more people searched for it, several more credible news agencies picked up the story, which was no longer about whether Ms. Wulff had her wild past, but whether Google is right in doing what it is doing.

When the case went to the court, Google argued, unsuccessfully, that its autosuggest is a neutral tool. It merely aggregates all the different things that people are searching for and helpfully gives them an overview of the most popular and trending search queries submitted by others in the hivemind (Kulish 2012).[20] The United Nations had run an entire campaign around this, using Google's autocomplete as a way to trace misogyny. However, as has been proven in other cases in France and Belgium, autosuggest is not as innocent as that. Data research has shown that autosuggest skillfully guides users to search for particular queries and influences what they eventually end up surfing for. Because, let's face it, if you ever searched for the name of your favorite celebrity, and see options that connect them to naked, prostitution, scandal, leaked tape, or any other hint of an *Eyes Wide Shut* moment, you are going to click on their name. And, ironically, the more you click on that autosuggest option, the more Google is going to argue that this is what people are searching for, and hence this should remain the top search result. Google autosuggest is, then, a self-fulfilling prophecy and has clear liability for the results that it is showing. Remember, that in the same year that Ms. Wulff was suing Google for libel, Google had already faced huge critique for its misogyny when it came to women in sciences. Because there was a time when, if you searched on Google for "women scientists," Google's helpful searchbot asked you, "Didn't you mean men scientists?" because obviously, if you are searching for women who were scientists, you just made a typo.

Google, in the court case in Germany, argued that it was presenting objective results based on its trend analysis of what users were looking for. However, it has been proven that Google's claims to objectivity are at least dubious. In the past, it has removed results that it has found to cause liability, especially toward minors. It has removed autocomplete suggestions when they encouraged competition with their own products. They have also succumbed to companies who have lobbied for autocomplete suggestions that harm their reputation (Lischka 2012).[21] And as Jennie Olofsson (2015) has shown in her research, Google has amplified biases by not only coding a different ranking system but by also mistaking "suggested clicks" as "organic search queries," thus steering its autocorrect and autocomplete features to guide user behavior. This was intentional lying, and covering up that lie through fake pretenses of objectivity, putting the responsibility of misogynist behavior back onto the users.

The story of Google and the unfortunate Bettina Wulff is important because it gives us a sense of the inversion that digital technologies produce about our histories, our futures, and our conditions of being a knowing subject. It is in its not knowing how it does what it does that Google was able to change the ways in which the history and future of Bettina Wulff was unfolding on the digital domain. On the one hand, Google was offering new histories for Wulff, without the evidence of historical fact. Based merely on hearsay and rumors, Google was able to override Wulff's own real-life incidents, her public protests, and her other material credentials to suggest that the only important history that Wulff will have to live with now is the one where she might be a prostitute or an escort. Even if Google does offer a public apology and changes its codes, a search result with Wulff's name in it is going to only show the fact that this sordid connection existed. This process is contrary to all our understanding of how histories get constructed: There is an event, and it leaves traces and evidences. These are recovered and stitched together through memory and desire to create narratives that explain who we are and why we are so. However, through the case of Ms. Wulff, Google has now made us aware that we are alienated from definitive histories.

We have become deterritorialized subjects who are so distributed, such organisms without organs, so swept up in the digital, that the only ontology, the only genesis, the only beginning and the only history we can now have is the one that the digital predicts for us. At the same time, as the autosuggest results show, the only futures that Wulff can have, in these search-engine-driven, information-saturation points, are the futures that Google can author for her. In other words, Google suddenly appears to have the capacity of predicting the past, thus making us perpetually fake, without any fidelity or fixity to the histories that we claim for ourselves.

To understand the inversion of time is also perhaps to understand the tension of thinking about the computation and fakeness through a trade-off between possibility and probability. This model argues that the computer is a mathematical device and that it embodies the quantum possibilities that mathematics embody. Within mathematics, any state of crisis has infinite and multiple outcomes, and when faced with a crisis—we are not talking about dramatic crises of things collapsing but the more banal crisis of having to make a choice every time multiple options emerge—the digital can compute all the possibilities and then make a choice about the next stop. This means that the computer actually is able to give voice to, recognize, and augment all the different possibilities—things that have not happened, things that cannot happen, things that would never happen, and give them all an *in-potentia* existence. Our histories are being opened up by the digital where all the choices that are possible, but not probable, are being explored, and different origin points are chosen to create us into different kinds of subjects.

This capacity of the digital that uses traces as evidence to predict the histories is at the heart of this argument on fakeness. In our nondigital representational modes, we have always thought of history as a given, as fixed, as determinate and produced through evidence. The future, on the other hand, was one that was filled with precariousness and possibility. It was unplanned and ineffable. The human subject was constructed as a creature of the past, tied to history, but unfettered from the future, and with the agency, autonomy, and choice to create its own future. This reworking of the past—call it either an emancipation from it or a revision of it—has consequences for the future as a scarce commodity.

However, with the digital we now have a new inversion where the future is already scripted, narrated; a few options are made available and those are the only ones that will be accepted. The way the future is narrated is by making history a game of prediction, where we are now able to produce new and intangible histories of the subject, through big-data correlations and through new modes of assembling our identities. And thus, we are reaching a stage where we cannot expect much from our future, because it is already appearing as a known entity, made legible and tame by the algorithmic protocols that are governing our lives. And at the same time, the histories that gave us validity, or some sense of endurance and memory, are quickly being eroded. In the result we are producing a subject who can have neither nostalgia nor aspiration, neither memory nor fantasy, and is left only with the everyday vision of an ever-expansive time—time that is no longer about the past or the future. There might have been a possible yesterday, there will be a possible tomorrow, and they are going to frame you—in every sense of that phrase—into the now, which can have no nostalgia for the past and no expectations of the future.

Old-Fashioned Ways of Doing Things

In the midst of all these convoluted musings on the twisted nature of time, the uncertain nature of truth, and the definite imperative of the fake, which our networks seem to create, there are still multiple ways out. I call it the old-fashioned ways of doing things.

It is in the nature of networks to segregate us. In order to connect, they first need to separate. In order to cluster, they first need to individuate. For efficient flow of information—to protect us from the information overload of ourselves—they need to group us into what Wendy HuiKyong Chun (2017) calls "networks of homophily," where we coexist with people who are like us, and have a healthy suspicion of people who are unlike us and hence are also polarized in their difference. Social media intensities and scaled incidents of violent communication have shown how, within these digital networks, we are separated by differences that appear insurmountable, even though our similarities are often larger than the sets of differences. However, for a network to function, it needs to create "small worlds" (Watts 1999), which keep us both immersed in and excluded from the large and overwhelming streams of networked information.

These are particularly visible when we encounter contentious human questions—about our bodies, our politics, our social organizations, and political processes. The difference is naturalized, presented to as the descriptors of our communication, and enabling disagreement without a dialogue, a fight without friendship, connectivities without collectivities. In India, where questions of gender and bodily justice have always encountered the paradoxes of modernity and intersections of distributed inequities, these conversations are fraught and furious, often generating prewired responses of denial, dismissal, or damnation. Digital claims of oppression are countered by digital claims of fakeness; activists are confronted by counteractivists; people who speak back, call out, resist, are intimidated, bullied, and silenced by the very technologies and platforms on which they seek to find freedom. The insistence on difference makes it impossible for any "truth claim" to go beyond the "consensual hallucination" of the filter bubbles that we are placed within.

And yet, we continuously see digitally mediated collectives emerge, occupy the space of consciousness raising, bringing many different alliances together and giving them platforms for visibility and voice. These are innovative, creative, distributed, and unprecedented, breaking through structural scripts and institutionalized biases. However, the ones that are the most effective are the ones that refuse to follow the logics of the networks and the mechanics of these digital scripts. They write their own narratives and mobilize the digital, not to create differences but to harness the similarities—generating conditions of affirmation over confrontation.

The Blank Noise Project is one of the longest standing and largest collaborative, crowdsourced digital platforms and communities of "action heroes" in India. The volunteers fight for gender and sexual justice in public spaces in India and have shown how the old-fashioned ideas of human collectives—often thought of as anachronistic and irrelevant, fake or infidel—remain relevant and critical to the new networked realities of our times. One of the

most startling examples of their successful programming is in a
project called "Talk To Me." The project encourages dialog with
these lines:

> Talk To Me, because fear is taught, transferred, inherited
> and can be unlearnt.
> Talk To Me because I am ready to question the politics
> of fear.
> Talk To Me so we can initiate possible friendships,
> connection, trust and empathy.[22]

Jasmeen Patheja, the founder and the visionary artist who has
built the Blank Noise Project and its large, distributed, digitally
connected community, worked with a team of volunteers at the
Srishti Institute of Art, Design, and Technology in Bangalore, India,
to identify that there are many streets and roads that are desig-
nated as "rapist lanes" in the country. These are lanes that, due to
their design, situatedness, and demographic location, are spaces
where women feel unsafe, and where aggressive harassment and
threats are naturalized.

The project mobilized volunteers to arrive on these lanes with
a table and two chairs, and instead of immediately shouting,
shaming, or fighting with men who might be creating these hostile
conditions—as we would have done in the call-out cultures we
have naturalized on Twitter—they invited them to come and have
a conversation about why they do what they do. Reporting on the
project, Leon Tan (2014) locates it in the tradition of feminist art
practices of the 1970s, where dialogue, time, and a capacity for
what Karen Barad (2007) calls "inter-action" become the focus of
framing and addressing the problem. Neither the experience of
the woman nor the action of the male harasser were thought of
as polarized and distinct, or invalidated or excused. There was a
genuine call to understand the multiple registers of our lives and
gendered relationships, and what emerged were long conversations, a generation of empathy, a catalysis of responsibility, and
through these very old-fashioned modes of digital engagement, the

lanes characteristically became some of the safest, where former harassers took it upon themselves to correct and change the nature of that public space.

The speed of internet time and the mandate of novelty that the attention networks come with often propel us in the quest of the new, dismissing the older forms as both aesthetically fake and politically irrelevant. It is easy to suggest that networks that are old (only in internet time—so like, three years ago) and practices that are not abreast of the latest social media fads are often neglected as without purpose, and the meanings and voices that come from them are often seen as unreliable because they do not mimic the design aesthetics and the trending modes of communication that make digital processes cutting edge and reliable. We can see this even in everyday practices—the posts that our parents and grandparents make on a social media network, the forwards that we receive on messaging apps from extended networks that haven't quite updated themselves on the new conditions of "future time" communication, and thus are immediately open to ridicule or rehabilitation. Organizations that cannot keep up with this continually updated packaging and appearing on resolutely new channels that make fake everything that came before them often find themselves struggling to find a meaningful communication of decades of work that is built by large communities.

"Talk To Me"is a great example of moving away from these snap judgments of datedness and fakeness that we deliver so easily. The Blank Noise Project community reminds us that, just because we use these digital technologies and networks, we do not have to follow the time and speed they prescribe. We can look at human temporalities and modes of doing. If we only found our own forms of reaching out, connecting, and communication, we would be able to find our own ways of claiming and validating truths. There will be multiple truths. They will be fragmented. They might even be contradictory. But they can coexist, not as a resolution but as a di-alogue where we do not simply toss things out as fake but instead carefully understand why they are being identified or dismissed as fake. As Alexandra Juhasz mentioned poignantly, in our conversa- tions while creating this book, *"all the rest would and continues to be invented in dialogue, technology, and time."*

It Is Not Fake if It Fools You

So this is where we are. Ending perhaps, at the same point where we began, but also, hopefully, inverting the questions that we began with. In the current obsession about fake, and the quest for determining the real truth, it is better to focus on the really fake. Because in the digital computational networks, truth is a negative category; it is what remains when all the fake has been subtracted from the information that is being analyzed. So we do not build determinants of truth, we build determinants to filter the fake, and these filters need to determine what is really fake.

The problem with the fake is that if it fools you, it is not a fake. The only way that something gets detected as really fake is that it deviates from its self-proclaimed purpose and meaning. However, human interactions and languages are imprecise, flawed, fractured, and subject to multiple meanings and rendering. Hence, human truths are often contextual, contingent, and contiguous, perhaps contagious. They do not depend on the omission of the fake but learn to integrate the fake into the stories of truth telling. Thus, when dealing with human factors of fakeness, we can accept the following statements to be all simultaneously and collectively true: Not all fake stories are lies. Not all lies are fake truths. Not all real stories are true. Not all truths are innocent of fakeness. In fact, we don't generally think of our lives as spliced through the edges of truths and lies. We negotiate with facts, fictions, fallacies, and fantasies, and mix them together to form complex values that give us space to be who we are, and we forget it when we need to.

The reason fakeness has become such a problem in the digitally mediated world is not because this negotiation with truth has changed in scale, scope, or time. It isn't as if all of us are suddenly telling more fibs than before, or that we are telling deeper and more profound lies, or telling them faster than we did earlier. Shaping fakeness as a digital condition often maps it on computational networks and presents it as a problem of technological proportions, with the human subject as incidental or non-agential. This leads to the staging of human truths versus technological truths, social lies versus networked facts, circulating untruths versus consolidated falsehoods, erring humans versus efficient machines. Rehearsing these arguments generates a cybernetic feedback loop that distances human experience from machine logic, forever presenting one or the other as fake.

Measure of Bodies That Measure Up

It is, in fact, a condition where we establish an uncertainty in our capacities to tell, discern, and understand information and make meaning. It is not about being fooled by the machine but about being no longer sure in our ability to tell the machine from the human. The real fakeness is not about loss of control over the information but our alienation from it. Really Fake is a condition where

> . . . information gets reduced to a spectacle,

> . . . memories get morphed into storage,

> . . . we find ourselves in states of indeterminacy

> . . . truths emerge as partial and also malleable,

> . . . we encounter the invalidation of collective truths by structurally empowered actors

> . . . things move in and out storage

> . . . people get punished for sharing and being shared into virality

> . . . our encounters with each other are marked by pastness

> . . . time no longer adheres to sequence of moments

. . . and we are fooled, not by the fakeness of the
information but by our distance from it.

This essay is an attempt to map that distance, to articulate that
alienation, to recognize and acknowledge the void that is growing
in our sense of self and the stories that are told about that self, and
the ways in which digital technologies are mining this distance and
perpetuating it, in order to become the de facto tools of shaping
our sense of the world. While these practices continue, distancing
us from each other, from ourselves, and from our memories, there
is still a possibility of measuring fake by making it as big as and no
bigger than our bodies and the worlds, commitments, humans,
and machines it can hold and is held by.[23] It is an attempt to show
how fakeness, when stretched across human scales of space, time,
and function, can be diffused. As we encounter fake news and its
poisonous polarizations, we remember that we have an antidote,
and that is in intimacy—with the information, with the media, with
the technologies—in stories, and in doing things with stories with
each other, to each other, and to ourselves.

Notes

1   In her chapter in this book, Alexandra Juhasz introduces this idea of authenti-
    cating a truth from another real time to think of our bodies as networks, and
    our analysis as cyberfeminists encountering the fake as inspired as much by
    poetry as it is rooted in experience and empirical data.

2   Maitrayee Chauduri (2012) in "Feminism in India: The Tale and Its Telling" does
    a masterful task of showing the tensions between "Women studies," "Women's
    rights work," and "Academic Feminism" as they emerge from different geneal-
    ogies and often exclude actors who might have similar goals but very different
    tactics and institutional practices that do not sit easily within any one of these
    boxes.

3   Liu Jen-peng and Ding Naifei (2006), in their influential essay "Reticent Poetics,
    Queer Politics," explore a different tone, register, and mode of queerness that
    does not have to follow the forcefully global aesthetic of queer "coming out."
    Originally published in Mandarin, the essay looks at how queerness needs to
    be situated as a collective and inextricably entangled set of filial and social
    relationships that do not offer the clean breakaway points of distinctly and
    discreetly queer desire and personhood.

4   Sara Ahmed, in her path-breaking book *The Promise of Happiness* (2010),

postulates the figure of the "Melancholic Migrant" to look at how the process of assimilation binds the migrant into being always happy, blissful about where they have landed, and always performing this happiness, as a sign of gratitude and reassurance, despite structural conditions of oppression and discrimination. It is important to hold onto this idea of fakeness as a form of legitimacy—performing an emotion that grants you acceptance—because it plays out in the shaping of multiple intersections of personhood, where we are continually told that we would make ourselves more accessible if only we "smiled a little more."

5 Alexandra Juhasz (2020), in her chapter in this book, reminds us that fakeness is not just a static aesthetic but also a fading and erasure of truth with the lapsing of time. It becomes important that fakeness is accrued and is often emerging from the misaligned temporalities of durability and duration of the different elements and actors involved in the process of making meaning.

6 In the prologue to the book *How We Became Posthuman,* N. Katherine Hayles (1999) picks up the "red-herring" of gender determination in Turing's proposition, to remind us, "What the Turing test 'proves' is that the overlay between the enacted and the represented bodies is no longer a natural inevitability but a contingent production, mediated by a technology that has become so entwined with the production of identity that it can no longer meaningfully be separated from the human subject. To pose the question of "what can think" inevitably also changes, in a reverse feedback loop, the terms of 'who can think'" (ix).

7 In her chapter in this book, Alexandra Juhasz, looking at the explosion of fake media and fake news on social media platforms, but particularly YouTube, argues that the tactics of faking involved a continued muddling of questions without any attempt at clarification. It is not fake that pretends to be real—it is a fake that disrupts the staging of the real without any intention of actually offering a way out of that moment of derailment.

8 In his chapter on "Queer Mobiles and Mobile Queers" (2017), Nishant Shah identifies how queerness in these instances is not just a condition of the body but also of the technology. The capacity for intimate digital devices to become extensions of our bodies, and in return shape our bodies in the new hashtag taxonomies that might be not "real" for the body but are "real" for the technological network and circulation, is worth keeping in mind.

9 William Gibson's iconic description, which still remains subject to multiple interpretations and speculations, in *Neuromancer* (1984), says: "Cyberspace. A consensual hallucination experienced daily by billions of legitimate operators, in every nation, by children being taught mathematical concepts . . . A graphic representation of data abstracted from banks of every computer in the human system. Unthinkable complexity. Lines of light ranged in the nonspace of the mind, clusters and constellations of data. Like city lights, receding . . ."

10 Sanrio offers clarification guidelines that say very clearly, "Hello Kitty was done in the motif of a cat. It's going too far to say that Hello Kitty is not a cat. Hello Kitty is a personification of a cat." In their response to a query from the online otaku fanzine *Kotaku,* Sanrio admitted that Hello Kitty is "gijinka'—an

anthropomorphization—but not a cat, while *she* is also definitely not, not a cat. Hence, like Snoopy is a dog even if *he* walks upright, Hello Kitty is still not a cat in the way in which Snoopy is a dog. This can go on for a while. I think it is good to stop here before we fall down a rabbit hole (https://kotaku.com/dont-be-silly-hello-kitty-is-a-cat-1627820750).

11   An archived version of the advertisement is available on https://www.youtube.com/watch?v=WhF7dQl4Ico.

12   In their Introduction to the *Routlege Companion to Global Histories* volume, Gerard Goggin and Mark McLelland (2016) remind us that the TCP/IP protocol is not just a circulation protocol but also a verification protocol: it determines what is and what is not the internet, and even in its hybrid forms, it continues to regulate the devices that can come in, after verification, and join the digital network and the devices that shall be excluded from going online.

13   In the paper 'Sluts 'r'us' (2015) I have argued that sluttiness, like many other instances of ascribed reality discussed in this essay, is a condition of fakeness. "Slut shaming is a prime example of the distributed and stealthy nature of agency in processes of configuration. Those identified as 'victims' of revenge pornography are sluts, not because they are necessarily engaged in slutty practices. In fact, most of them are defined as 'good' women engaged in intimate activities with men whom they trust. They become 'slutty' as their images migrate and reproduce by the perpetual memory machine of the Web."

14   Emily Greenhouse (2014), writing for *The New Yorker,* presents a compelling narrative of the case and unravels the ways by which the legal data-protection regulations helped regulate and eventually shut down the activities of Hunter Moore and his network of harmful, nonconsensual pornographic circulation.

15   Alexandra Juhasz, in her chapter in this book, argues that there is a "feminist cybermethod of validation" that goes beyond the technological verification that often supersedes the bodily over the data, and I want to imagine that this essay is a way of puncturing this machine-driven narrative to offer a feminist reading of fakeness.

16   In her inspiring and insightful lecture *Post-archive: Scholarship in the Digital Age* at Brown University, Mcpherson shows how the digital has changed the archive to become "everywhere" and how it needs to be reanimated by "injecting the human" and stopping the database and algorithmic culture of archiving as the default truth. The lecture is available at https://www.youtube.com/watch?v=i5g Js8sEQRg&feature=emb_logo. In her book *Feminist in a Software Lab,* Mcpherson (2018) particularly offers "Intersectionality, the cut, collaboration, fuzzy edges, entanglement, and assemblages" (276) as ways by which feminist materialist and queer-of-color practices can interrupt the otherwise straightforward notion of archiving as memory.

17   While there are many different reports and analyses of this LoSHA, I find Sara Morais dos Santos Bruss's (2019) analysis of it as infrastructure of parrhesia—whistleblowing, a critically urgent formulation to enter this debate. Bruss categorically helps understand that the digital list was not just a question of what we can believe or not—a question of fake and true—but more a question

of how we tell truth in the mediated environments of digital networks. Bruss helps move the debate from "good list–bad list" to examining the conditions within which the truth of the list transcends the factual verification imperatives put upon it.

18 Alexandra Juhasz, in her essay in this book, positions datedness as a feminist intervention to deal with time that otherwise stamps a definite truth (or fakeness) value onto objects that can be dismissed easily as irrelevant because of their existence outside of immediate time.

19 Donna Haraway's (1991) spectacular postulation that the cyborg is part fantasy, part fiction, and part reality has always inspired me to think not only about fantasies of a cyborg future but about cyborg fantasies of a human future, and it is a point worth driving home.

20 Writing for the *New York Times,* Nicholas Kulish quotes the spokesperson for Google in Germany, Kay Oberbeck, saying, "All of the queries shown in Autocomplete have been typed previously by other Google users."

21 Konrad Lischka, writing for *Der Spiegel,* charts out how Google has manipulated its "neutral" results in the past to protect its business interests, but clearly the clickbait nature of this autocorrect is in the interest of Google's traffic and hence it refused to intervene in this instance.

22 From the project description of "Talk To Me" by the Blank Noise Project. Along with "Talk To Me," there are many other Blank Noise Project initiatives that can be accessed at http://www.blanknoise.org/talk-to-me.

23 In her chapter in this book, Alexandra Juhasz produces this formulation as a design principle that helps map out the "escape routes" that allow for cyberfeminist truths in the field of machine fakery. She does it with poetry. I do it with stories.

References

Ahmed, Sara. 2010. *The Promise of Happiness.* Durham, N.C.: Duke University Press.

Arun, Chinmayi. 2019. "On WhatsApp, Rumours, Lynchings, and the Indian Government." *Economic & Political Weekly* 54, no. 6: https://www.epw.in/journal/2019/6/insight/whatsapp-rumours-and-lynchings.html.

Barad, Karen. 2007. *Meeting the Universe Halfway: Quantum Physics and the Entanglement of Matter and Meaning.* Durham, N.C.: Duke University Press.

Bruss, Sara Morais dos Santos. 2019. "Naming and Shaming or 'Speaking Truth to Power'? On the Ambivalences of the Indian 'List of Sexual Harassers in Academia' (LoSHA)." *Ephemera Theory and Politics in Organization*: http://www.ephemerajournal.org/contribution/naming-and-shaming-or-%E2%80%98speaking-truth-power%E2%80%99-ambivalences-indian-%E2%80%98list-sexual-0.

Chakraborty, Arpita. 2019. "Politics of #LoSHA: Using Naming and Shaming as a Feminist Tool on Facebook." *Gender Hate Online* , ed. Debbie Ging and Eugenia Siapera; https://doi.org/10.1007/978-3-319-96226-9_10.

Chauduri, Maitrayee. 2012. "Feminism in India: The Tale and Its Telling." *Revue Tiers Monde* 209, no. 1: 19–36; https://doi.org/10.3917/rtm.209.0019.

Chun, Wendy HuiKyong. 2006. *Control and Freedom: Power and Paranoia in the Age of Fiber Optics.* Cambridge, Mass.: MIT Press.

Chun, Wendy HuiKyong. 2017. *Updating to Remain the Same: Habitual New Media* Cambridge, Mass.: MIT Press.

Dibbell, Julian. 1993. "A Rape in Cyberspace, or How an Evil Clown, a Haitian Trickster Spirit, Two Wizards, and a Cast of Dozens Turned a Database into a Society." *The Village Voice,* 21 December : http://www.juliandibbell.com/texts/bungle_vv.html.

Gajalla, Radhika, ed. 2013. *Cyberculture and the Subaltern: Weavings of the Virtual and the Real.* Plymouth: Lexington Books.

Gibson, William. 1984. *Neuromancer.* New York: Ace Books.

Goggin, Gerard, and Mark McLelland, eds. 2016. "Introduction: Global Coordinates of Internet Histories." *Routledge Companion to Global Histories.* New York: Routledge.

Greenhouse, Emily. 2014. "The Downfall of the Most Hated Man on the Internet." *The New Yorker:* https://www.newyorker.com/tech/annals-of-technology/the-downfall-of-the-most-hated-man-on-the-internet.

Haraway, Donna. 1991. "A Cyborg Manifesto: Science, Technology, and Socialist Feminism in the Late Twentieth Century." In *Simians, Cyborgs, and Women: The Reinvention of Nature.* New York: Routledge.

Hayles, N. Katherine. 1999. "Introduction." In *How We Became Posthuman: Virtual Bodies in Cybernetics, Literature, and Informatics.* Chicago: University of Chicago Press.

Jonze, Spike. 2013. *Her.* Film. Warner Bros. Pictures.

Kulish, Nicholas. 2012. "As Google Fills in Blank, a German Cries Foul." *The New York Times:* https://www.nytimes.com/2012/09/19/world/europe/keystrokes-in-google-bare-shocking-rumors-about-bettina-wulff.html.

Lee, Dave. 2012. "IsAnyoneUp's Hunter Moore: 'The Net's Most Hated Man.'" *BBC*: http://www.bbc.com/news/technology-17784232.

Lischka, Konrad. 2012. "Defamation Case Highlights Google's Double Standards." *Spiegel International*: https://www.spiegel.de/international/germany/defamation-case-by-bettina-wulff-highlights-double-standard-at-google-a-854914.html.

Liu, Jen-peng, and Naifei Ding. 2006. "Reticent Poetics, Queer Politics." *Inter-Asia Cultural Studies* 6, no. 1: 30–55; https://doi.org/10.1080/1462394042000326897.

Losh, Elizabeth. 2017. "All Your Base Are Belong to Us: Gamergate and Infastructures of Online Violence." *Fieldsights,* April 28: https://culanth.org/fieldsights/all-your-base-are-belong-to-us-gamergate-and-infrastructures-of-online-violence.

McPherson, Tara. 2018. *Feminist in a Software Lab: Difference + Design.* Cambridge, Mass.: Harvard University Press.

Menon, Nivedita. 2017. "Statement by Feminists on Facebook Campaign to "Name and Shame." *Kafila*: https://kafila.online/2017/10/24/statement-by-feminists-on-facebook-campaign-to-name-and-shame/.

Olofsson, Jennie. 2015. "Did You Mean 'Why Are Women Cranky?' Google—A Means of Inscription, a Means of De-inscription." In *Between Humanities and the Digital,* ed. Patrik Svensson and David Theo Goldberg, 243–52. Cambridge, Mass.: MIT Press.

Ongley, Jeela. 2014. "Hello Kitty Revelation from Manoa Anthropologist Christine Yano Shakes up the Internet." *University of Hawai'i News*: https://www.hawaii.edu/news/2014/08/28/hello-kitty-revelation-from-manoa-anthropologist-christine-yano-shakes-up-the-internet/.

Philip, Kavita. 2005. "What Is a Technological Author? The Pirate Function and Intellectual Property." *Postcolonial Studies* 8, no. 2: 199–218; https://doi.org/10.1080/13688790500153596.

Rochefort, Simone de. 2017. "Twitch Is Home to Two Google Home Devices Debating the Existence of God: So . . . Singularity?" *Polygon*: https://www.polygon.com/2017/1/6/14192494/google-home-assistant-debate-the-existence-of-god-twitch.

Scholz, Trebor, ed. 2013. *Digital Labor: The Internet as Playground and Factory.* New York: Routledge.

Shah, Nishant. 2015. "Sluts 'r' Us: Intersections of Gender, Protocol, and Agency in the Digital Age." *First Monday* 20, no. 4: http://dx.doi.org/10.5210/fm.v20i4.5463.

Shah, Nishant. 2017. "Queer Mobiles and Mobile Queers: Intersections, Vectors, and Movements in India." In *Routledge Handbook of New Media in Asia,* ed. Larissa Hjorth, and Olivia Khoo, 275–84. London: Routledge.

Shankar, Karthik, and Raya Sarkar. 2017. "Why I Published a List of Sexual Predators in Academia." *Buzzfeed News*: https://www.buzzfeed.com/karthikshankar/why-i-published-a-list-of-sexual-predators-in-academia.

Tan, Leon. 2014. "Talk to Me." *Institute for Public Art*: https://www.instituteforpublicart.org/case-studies/talk-to-me/.

Tsou, YiPing (Zona). 2015. "From 'Flash Mob' to 'Human Flesh Search.'" In *Digital Activism in Asia Reader,* ed. Nishant Shah, Sneha Puthiya Purayil, and Sumandro Chattapadhyay, 179–96. Lüneburg: meson press.

Turing, Alan M. 1950. "Computing Machinery and Intelligence." *Mind* 54: 433–57.

Watts, Duncan. 1999. *Small Worlds: The Dynamics of Networks between Order and Randomness.* Princeton, N.J.: Princeton University Press.

Zuckerman, Ethan. 2008. "The Cute Cat Theory Talk at ETech." http://www.ethanzuckerman.com/blog/2008/03/08/the-cute-cat-theory-talk-at-etech/.

Authors

Alexandra Juhasz is distinguished professor of film at Brooklyn College, CUNY. Her books include *Women of Vision: Histories in Feminist Film and Video,* coedited with Jesse Lerner (Minnesota, 2001), *F Is for Phony: Fake Documentary and Truth's Undoing* (Minnesota, 2006) and *Learning from YouTube*.

Ganaele Langlois is associate professor in communication studies at York University, Canada, and associate director of the Infoscape Centre for the Study of Social Media (www.infoscapelab.ca). She is author of *Meaning in the Age of Social Media* and coeditor of *Compromised Data: From Social Media to Big Data*.

Nishant Shah is director of research and outreach and professor of aesthetics and cultures of technology at the ArtEZ University of the Arts, The Netherlands. He is coeditor of *Digital Activism in Asia Reader* (meson press, 2015).